ACCEPTANCE

Published by Spines
ISBN: 979-8-89569-306-3

ACCEPTANCE

TIME

JIMMY MARSHALL

**A MANUSCRIPT BY
JIMMY L. MARSHALL**

Marshall, Jimmy
Pine Bluff, Arkansas
2024

This book is dedicated to the following people for their invaluable contributions to my life:

Shellie Ross
Charlie Marshall Sr
Sydonia Harts
Willie Harts
Brenda Kaye Marshall

"Jim, thank you for your friendship. Come and see our state when you can..."

Denise, Utah

"Jim, be good..."

Ernest, Texas.

"Jimmy, I wish you the best from the bottom of my heart..."

Darlene, Texas

"Jim, thanks for the advice, T I M E (Things I Must Earn). Good luck."

Evan, Lynn Mass

"Jim, keep the sun to your face and the wind at your back."

Richard B, Lynn Mass

"Jimmy from Arkansas, best of luck; you can do it."

Love Kim

"Jimmy, good luck, and put the conditioner units in the lead. Haha. I do wish you all the best and hope you win the tournament."

Garry, D., Texas

"In five minutes, you taught me the meaning of life. Thank you forever. You know how you are."

Scott M, Utah

"Jimmy, you are the coolest person from Arkansas I have ever met. Love ya lots."

Tiffany (THANKS), Utah

"Jim, I have enjoyed your passion, direct approach, and honesty. I also appreciate your knowledge of your barriers and coping strategies, especially when they work against you. I believe you have imparted and enriched people more than you know. I was always assured of a good group when you were there. I appreciate your gifts."

Staff, Michele C. (LCSW), Utah

"Jimmy, it was great getting to know you. If you are ever in St. George, Utah, call me."

Kelly S., St. George, Utah

"It's been a pleasure meeting you, Jimmy. I wish you the best of luck."

Chad H.

"Jimmy, I have had a great time with you. Thanks for making me laugh and giving me the occasional reality check! Take care of yourself."

Sue. K., Bountiful, Utah

"Wishing you all the best. You are a great guy, and I know you are strong."

Cindy N. Palace Station, Las Vegas

"Jimmy, you are one of the wisest men I have ever met. If you are ever up my way and need anything, give me a call."

jusin M., Kemmerer, WY

"Jimmy, I have learned a lot from you. You are a natural leader. All the best to you."

Rich B.

"Jimmy, you will never know how much you've helped me. I will never let my memories of this time go because it will help me stay sober. I really have listened to you about letting go of the past. We had some good laughs. Also, I wish you the best, and may your HP always be with you. Let's keep in touch. A friend always."

Deb F.

"Jim, it's been a pleasure and an honor to have met you. I have respected your work ethic and your honesty. You are too good a man to let this bump in the road get you down. You can do it! Godspeed. One day at a time."

Jon S., Midway, Utah

"Jimmy, it's been a pleasure and an honor to know you, my friend. The best of luck to you. Keep it simple and take it one day at a time."

Michael G.

"Jimmy, I have had a lot of laughs and some sorrows, but all in all, we can see the end of the tunnel. It's clear and bright on the outside. It has been a pleasure knowing you will do just fine because of your strength and attitude. You have it all together. I hope part of me is going with you. Good luck. Godspeed."

Jim T., Utah

"Jimmy, stay in charge; your inner self is the answer."

Bruce, Utah

"Jim, you had a lot of advice for the younger kids. Let's hope we older guys can follow our own advice."

Bob R., Chicago, IL

"Jimmy, the promises (PG-83-84) are real. I am living proof. You are such a beautiful man, and I truly hope you will give yourself a chance. Call once in a while and let me know how you are doing. I truly wish you the best in everything. Take care."

Staff, Susan

"To Jimmy, a guy I met in rehab: I had a good time. Real therapy. Take care and be easy."

Dover, Ohio

"Jimmy, you are a good leader and have some insightful info. Also, you were a friend, and I enjoyed our trip to the big city of Salt. If you make it out this way again, give me a shout. Best of luck."

Mick C., Standbsy Park, Utah

"Jimmy, when you get that feeling that you want to use, make a phone call first. You know what you need to do. God bless."

Fred

"Jim, you're the man. Thanks for your friendship, your leadership, and all the nice compliments. I have faith that you will do great. You keep the faith that you can and will do great because you are a great man."

Shelly D. Aberdeen, Idaho

"Jim, I cannot thank you enough for your honesty and love! You have been more than a doctor or counselor by helping me understand what I need to be a man. I will never forget you and your sincerity." "I will also remember to be responsible for my actions." "I have confidence in your sobriety. You can make it. I feel that during the times we talked, my dad was talking to me." "It was not always what I wanted to hear." "...but I needed to hear it and recognize my issues." "That's the only way I can improve." It's true; I can't do this on my own, and I couldn't have done it without you. Thanks again for your love, care, and advice."

Michael W.

"Jimmy, the first step in this lifelong process is admitting. I think you have done that. It's simple, really, and all you need to do is change your using behaviors into healthy spiritual, mental, emotional, and physical ones. It's all or nothing. You either can do it, or you can't. I hope you do. You're worth it. I wish we lived in the same city." "I like hanging out with you." "You have been my Big Brother and called it like it was." "You made me feel good when

I was down." "I am going to miss you." We both know what's ahead of us: reality. Just do what you've got to do. You will be all right. Your friend. Call me."

Mike T.

"Big Jim, my man! We had some good times up in Hell. I am going to make this short and sweet because I know we will stay in touch. Without you and two more guys, I would not have gotten my s*** together! Thanks for your stories and advice. You believed in me. Thanks. Good luck, bro!"

Steve W., Salt Lake, Utah

Introduction

"Crack cocaine" makes the illusion of free will vanish. Most of your money is spent on ways to use it. In the long run, the only use happening is you using the people who love you. They could be family or friends. You lose conception of your values for family, job, self, religion, and anything else of value. If someone had told me this before I took my first hit of crack cocaine over 20 years ago, maybe my life for the past years would have been different—or maybe not.

Out of all the teachings there are, some things are best learned when an individual finds out on his or her own. It's a hard lesson sometimes, but I believe we, as humans, are destined to go through certain things, whether we want to or not. I believe this is how our faith is tested, if we have faith at all.

I am inviting you to go back into my life at a point where it became unbearable and unmanageable because of my drug usage. Read my stories where I lied, I cheated, and I even stole. It's a shame some of the things I did because of the addiction. We have the same similarities, such as hopelessness, helplessness, and life being unmanageable.

Now, I am not a suit-and-tie person who makes a living on Wall Street. You know, investing in stocks and bonds. I am not a millionaire who had it all and lost it all. And I am not your superstar athlete who gets paid big bucks to excite crowds with his athletic ability. I am just your average, everyday person who has a good-paying job and a belief in family and God.

My story isn't just about my drug use, although it was a significant part of my problem; it focuses on my family's struggles to cope with me and my clinging to my addiction. This story also addresses some of the insanity and guilt that I went through mentally. I'm warning you: this is not a story about sex and violence. Even though there is death and destruction—the death of my spirituality and the destruction of my mind—this story is about change.

A person's willingness to change and become submissive. They say everybody has a story, so here's mine. We, as addicts, are blinded by our own way of thinking. Have you ever tried to hide money from yourself? It is impossible to do that! We have used everyone else, so now we start working on ourselves. We start trying to fool ourselves first, and that's where the head games come in; it's nothing but trickery. Somehow, we think we can change the design of how things work in our lives or how they ought to be. We attempt to self-medicate by using smaller doses. We hide our money, convincing ourselves we don't have a problem by comparing our usage to someone who has hit rock bottom. We focus on what we have instead of what we've lost. Some dwell on what they have lost instead of what they have, picking one over the other.

The difference between our problems and our solutions is *acceptance*.

Author's Autobiography

I was born on January 15th, 1952, in Plum Bayou, Arkansas, a little community outside of Tucker, Arkansas. My parents were Shellie Ross and Charlie Marshall. I have never seen a picture of my mother at all; many people describe her, and their descriptions are all different. I barely remember my father; he was never really around me growing up as a child, even though we lived in the same town. My mother and father were not married at the time of my birth or any other time, as far as that is concerned.

I have heard people say that my mother promised me to Mrs.Sydonia Harts; everyone called her Mrs. C. She had a kind and gentle soul, and her husband was Will Harts. He worked as a sharecropper. He was a hard-working man.

As fate would have it, my mother passed away. She was about 34 years old. I was about a year and a half old when this took place. Will and Sydonia Harts became my foster parents. Later in life, I discovered that I had other brothers and sisters. As it turns out, I had ten siblings—some on my father's side and some on my mother's side. I had two sisters, Joyce and Birthola (on my mother's side), who were raised by an aunt. It would be nearly 13 years before I would see them; in fact, Joyce and I could pass for twins. May Joyce (2007) rest in peace. To be honest, I never knew I had sisters. The truth was my foster parents didn't want relatives to know because they feared relatives would come and take me away. I was not adopted. Will and Sydonia just took me and raised me, and I thank God for that. They had no children of their own. Will and Sydonia Hart were outstanding parents. They gave me the best of what they had ... love.

My brothers (mother's side) lived with different people in a small town called Sherrill, Arkansas, the town my mother had moved to before she died. The best I can remember is that my dad passed away when I was 8 years old. He was a Marshall, Charlie Marshall.

"What's confusing is I went to school as a Hart (Will and Sydonia) and graduated as a Hart. In fact, Jimmy Marshall never technically went to school."

I was raised on a farm in the fifties and sixties. A lot of work was done by manual labor; they say you have not worked until you have worked on a farm. I agree.

When I became of age, I did my share of picking and chopping cotton; before that, my parents would leave me at a neighbor's house while they worked the fields. I was a fat, chubby kid; yeah, I loved to eat anything that was sweet and meaty; that's how I got the name Fat Man. The name Fat Man stuck with me for years; I guess it's better than being called Cookie Mouth. Growing up, kids had nicknames.

My parents were church-going people; neither one had much education, but that did not dampen their belief in God. My mother made sure I went to two places: church

2

and school, and I thank her for it. When it came to drinking, they drank socially on Saturdays, leading into Saturday night. I can truly say I don't recall seeing them drink on any other day of the week. You see, after working all week, on the weekend, you kind of let your hair down. Drinking was the way it was done.

I can close my eyes now and see all the smoke-filled cafes, the smell of cooking fish and hamburgers, the laughter in the air, and music playing from the jukeboxes; even for a child, those were the good days. I remember the two old guys just getting sloppy drunk and falling all over the place; as kids, it tickled us. Little did we know that they had a problem. Every Saturday, they were full of it, staggering all over the place and bumping into each other. Their clothes were soiled from spilled liquor and urine, and dirty from falling on the ground. A lot of people seemed to be having a good time.

I remember having my first drink of hard liquor, not to mention sipping on homemade wine that my mother would make. Yes, she made homemade wine from grapes, and she would give me some on occasion. My first strong drink was Johnny Walker Red. I was about fourteen or fifteen years old. It burned like fire going down. Why would anybody in their right mind want to drink that stuff? That's why, even today, I am not much of a drinker of hard liquor; I don't touch the stuff; just give me beer instead.

I often think about the times my daddy said they would give me wine just to catch me stumbling all over the place. He said it was their form of entertainment since we had no television. How cruel. Back in those days, it was a common sight to go to the back of stores and see people drinking and gambling. That's how it was on the weekend back in those days, in my eyes. I had an older brother, and his name was Leon. Now Leon was one Cool Cat. He reminded me of a black Fonzie from Happy Days. He wore what was called a process, yes, process. A process is when a black man gets his hair straightened to look like white folks' hair. I never had a process but have always wanted one.

Leon was cool—starched and ironed jeans with big cuffs, a rolled up sleeved shirt with the collar popped, and a pack of cigs in his rolled shirt sleeve, with a cigarette behind the ear... Now, how cool is that? Yes, Leon was my hero. He was not around all the time, but he was someone I looked up to. He always recognized me as his baby brother, and I liked that. Leon died the way he lived: hard. He was a fighter. I mean, he would fight your butt at the drop of a hat for anyone who knew him. He had spent time locked up in jail on numerous occasions, and he spent a few years in the penitentiary for shooting a man, the wrong man. Like I said, he lived hard. In 1975, he was stabbed to death. May he rest in peace.

The parents who raised me had no other children, but from listening to them, I see that they had raised kids before. They were loving and sweet. Being their only child had its advantages and disadvantages. The advantage was that I didn't have to share food or toys. The disadvantage is that I got blamed sometimes for things I didn't do. I got a few memorable whippings, mostly for lying. My mother would always say, I am not whipping you for what you did; I am whipping you for lying about it; it didn't matter. They both hurt just the same, in my opinion. I was not a bad child growing up. I was very obedient. My parents may have been short on education but long on discipline. My father seldom did the whipping. He left that to the

Enforcer, my mother. I was a loner, somewhat like I am today. I learned to avoid really serious trouble. I got more whippings for eating and lying about it than I did for anything. I would literally drink syrup and eat sugar and drink up all the buttermilk. I had to live up to my reputation, Fat Man.

That reminds me of our neighbor named Mrs Gary. She had two cows that gave milk. People would come from miles around to get butter and buttermilk; I love buttermilk today. Mrs Gary made butter in the old-fashioned way by churning. She charged 35 cents per gallon. Mrs. Gary lived about a mile away from where I did. On a hot summer day, her cold buttermilk hit the spot. I remember my mother sending me a gallon of milk to get. Going was not a problem, but coming back was because I had the buttermilk. Cold buttermilk on a hot summer day. The temptation was there to stop and get myself a drink... and I made a big mistake because I drank more than usual. When I got home, my mother asked me if I had drunk any milk. I said no, my mother said you are lying. I started pleading my case. Little did I know that when I turned the milk bucket up to drink, I spilled some on my shirt. My mother wasted no time whipping my butt for that lie, and yeah, it was worth it. I never got a whipping; I didn't need it. At least, that's how my mother saw it. Old-fashioned whippings kept your butt out of trouble. Today, I appreciate every whipping I get, whether it is needed or not.

My parents believed in me going to school; they made sure I did, and I made sure I went. Going to school kept me out of the cotton fields. I wasn't about to miss any day of school; I knew the consequences. From the first to the twelfth grade, I stayed in the top five in my class, made the honor roll a time or two, and had perfect attendance. I would go to school sick to keep from working in the fields.

Growing up in the country, I was not exposed to a lot of outside elements. We did not get a television until I was a junior in high school. Television back then was nothing like it is today; my old little world was everything to me. We had this swing on our front porch. I would sit in that swing and pretend it was a car and go anywhere in the world—well, not anywhere in the world because I didn't know of many places to go, but it was fun pretending. Life was so simple to me back then.

Never did I hear my parents having a knockdown, drag-out argument, but from time to time, words would fly, mostly out of my mother's mouth. My dad was a quiet man; he very seldom argued back with my mother. He was a simple man with very little education, but he could read and write. He was a hard worker, but he did his share of drinking on the weekend; never the sloppy drunk type, but he would get full. I say that to say this: he never showed anger against me or my mom; he never raised his hand against me or her. He was a man for whom I have nothing but respect. To take a child in and raise him as your own and show him love says a lot, and I thank him (Will Hart).

They tell me that my biological father truly had a drinking problem. Some go as far as to say it likely took a few years off his life. I believe he lived into his late sixties. Living during the time he did took its toll. Now, with my understanding of drugs and alcohol, I am sure it affected his health. I don't know much about my biological mother. I've been told she died about a year after I was born. The mother who raised me was more of a social drinker. I never saw her drunk, but on the weekends, she would party, too; she loved her Miller High Life beer and snuff.

She was a wine server for some of the white farmers during the holidays, like Thanksgiving and Christmas.

Holidays were always fun for me because they meant cooking and eating. My mother was a good cook, and I was a good eater; that is how I got the name Fat Man. Also, she would slip me a little taste of the homemade wine. I weighed over 90 pounds in the 4th grade. I was a fat kid, but my weight never bothered me like it does today.

During my high school years, I started to slim down and lose weight. My weight became an asset when I played football. I also participated in track. I wasn't great at basketball, but I was quick on the football field. When I graduated from high school, I weighed 205 pounds and was probably the second largest person on campus, though some of my classmates might disagree. I attended a small country school, J.S. Walker High, in Wabbaseka, Arkansas. I graduated in 1970, along with 31 others in my class. I guess one of my biggest disappointments in life was not receiving a football scholarship when my coach promised I would. I felt I should have gotten a scholarship. On senior day, three other classmates put in applications to work for the railroad. Little did I know that the application would shape my future.

I will never forget Michael Robinson, my classmate. He had this white Ford pickup truck; he would come to pick me and another classmate, Willie Jay, up on a Friday night. All 3 of us were underage, but we would find someone to get us some liquor, basically some Boone's Farm Wine. For us country boys, that was the wine. Once we got it, we would ride down those country roads, just boozing away; we called it fun. We never got drunk because it would be a whipping if our parents found out we were drinking. Our parents were pretty strict. They believed in attending church, going to school, and respecting elders, be they white or black. All three of us are alive today. Michael has lost his eyesight, and Willie Jay lives in a nearby city. He is retired from the same railroad where I retired, but in a different city.

My first job in the city was with Goodyear, a few years before I went to the railroad. I came from the farm and went to work at Goodyear, making about 80 dollars a week changing tires, and I became good at it. The truth be told, that beat the hell out of driving a tractor from sunup to sundown six and a half days a week, eating dust all day, every day. But driving a tractor beat chopping and picking cotton; I had my share of both.

By now, my horizon was expanding. I was meeting people who lived in the city of Pine Bluff, and my level of fun was getting an upgrade. I looked forward to every weekend. I still lived at home, so I gave my parents money to help with household stuff. I managed to save a little while still having fun—all on just 80 dollars a week—Oh, how times will change!

They say life has a lot to do with timing and being in the right place at the right time. I stopped at a local radio station (KCAT) to put in a request for some people from my hometown of Sherrill, AR. Sherrill and Pine Bluff, AR, were only about 20 minutes apart. To me, that's a jump, hop, and a skip. In other words, it's not that far. The on-air DJ told me to read a script; he thought I had a good voice; how would I like to become a DJ? I said sure, not really knowing what a DJ really does. He gave me more information and told me they would be doing some training on how to take the test and get my FCC license. I did my studying, passed the test, got my FCC license, and got a job at a radio station as a disc jockey. To you, that's a

DJ. My on-air persona was the Music Man. I went from the Fat Man to the Music Man.

A Disc Jockey? Boy, was I excited! You bet I was. I felt like a kid in a candy store. I had seen DJs before give record hops at some of the juke joints in the country. I noticed how all the girls were excited over them. Back in the '70s, being a DJ was a big deal, hot stuff. Hell, with all the benefits, I would have done it for free. Well, truthfully speaking, the only benefits were meeting girls and free drinks because the pay was not great, but it was fun. As they say, don't quit your day job.

At one point in my life, in the early years after graduation, I thought I would end up in California. I had a brother who lived there. I really had dreams of living there, but those dreams never materialized. Pine Bluff was about as far as I made it. It seems I am attached, like an umbilical cord, to my birthplace, Sherrill, Arkansas. Having been raised in the country, I really had no big desire for city lights. Lots of people I knew left the country and went to bigger cities, but over the years, they returned. Farm work was beginning to play out in the 70s; picking and chopping cotton by hand was really a thing of the past; machinery was taking over....Times were changing.

I moved out on my own at 17 and vowed I would never move back. But there were times I wished I were back home; really, things got testy. I had a pretty good job; in fact, I had two jobs at the radio station and Goodyear. I was making decent money. But my desire to party and have a good time outweighed my paycheck. For the next 20 years, boy, did I do a lot of partying. The '70s and '80s were the party years.

I was losing personal possessions because I was not taking care of personal business, had poor money management, and was living above my means. I lost a car back in the '70s, not paying my bills, not being responsible, just plain stupid.

They say there are stages you go through before you become an addict or alcoholic; I think mine began in the seventies. Those stages were the casual user to the abuser; I was beginning to fit the bill. I went through those stages. It's amazing how we can actually look back on our lives and see where we got off track and where we went wrong. One of the biggest issues with me was that I never got back on track. I did make adjustments; I slowed my roll a little. I never was much of a drinker. Even today, I do very little drinking.

I always felt I was young enough to recover, but that was an illusion within itself. I was not mature enough to recover. I did not have the smarts, the willpower, or the know-how to recover; I was just rolling along like a log down a river, going wherever the current would take me. None of the things I learned in high school prepared me for the life I was living in the present. Sure, I was having fun; I was only living for the day that I woke up. I was not going to church anymore, living day by day. But let me tell you, I never forgot how I was raised. My mother's words would often resonate in my head: Don't run with bad company. She stressed that religiously, along with other godly values.

In April of 1972, things changed. Remember I told you on senior day that I put in an application with the railroad? Well, in April of 1972, I got that call from the railroad, and I got hired. Getting a job at the railroad was what every man wanted, young or old. Yes, things are starting to look up for this old country. I went from 80 dollars a week to over 300 dollars per week, and I also had a job working at a cotton gin at night. I had no problem working. I was raised in a working environment. My daddy, who raised me, was a hard worker. He worked the cotton fields in the daytime and the rice fields at night, plus we had sharecropped 21. Yeah, I know about working. My mother and I worked the 21 acres mainly by ourselves; she worked tirelessly every day. Cooked, washed clothes, and raised a garden. Yeah, she was tough. God bless her soul.

I moved from the country town of Sherrill to the city of Pine Bluff; I moved in with my sister and her husband. I can't say that was a mistake, but some of the events that took place, I believe, shaped my life. Well, for one reason, my brother-in-law smoked those funny-smelling cigarettes that made your eyes red, made you giggle, and if that wasn't enough, it made you eat everything in sight. Those were the seventies. Smoking pot was an acceptable thing to do, and I began as an old country boy who wanted to be accepted. Little did I know this would lead to other things. My sister's and my favorite brother-in-law's marriage broke up; back then, I could not understand why, but later on in life, I learned the reason. I feel his drinking was a big strain on the marriage. Today, I can see the self-destruction he was causing. I could see then that I didn't want to be like my brother-in-law, but it was cool being his roommate. He and I are close today, like little brother and big brother. We see each other from time to time and phone each other on occasion. I believe that today, we have a better understanding of and respect for one another.

I met my first wife in 1975 while I was working as a manager of a liquor store—yes, a liquor store. Before that, I worked as a salesman for Western Auto, and I was also a DJ for a local nightclub. A club called Mother Finest was the place to be to party. Free drinks and girls are just what the doctor ordered for the DJ—getting paid and having fun. What happens to the railroad? Well, in 1974, I lost my job at the railroad; nobody to blame but myself for not taking care of my responsibilities as an employee. Too much time taken off and not coming to work on time. I accept that. It is part of acceptance.

My first wife and I got married in the late seventies. We lived together for a total of seven years. Things for me had gotten better financially. I had finally gotten my job back at the railroad. Thank God for the union. My wife, at the time, was going to college; she got her degree and started teaching.

I was doing well at the railroad, and yes, I was still DJing at Mother Finest. Some of the people I hung out with or associated with smoked pot. Sometimes, I think we just lived to get high. It became an everyday thing for me. All my friends got high. I even got high at church_let's say what little church I attended; I got high on the job. In fact, I would go to work knowing I was going to smoke there. I loved my job. During that period, it was the norm; my best connections were at work.

In 1984, things began to change for me. It was the beginning of my downward spiral, not that things had not started earlier. My wife and I divorced several years ago. We had no children, so the divorce was a smooth operation. She is alive today and doing well. We speak on social media from time to time. Society as a whole started cracking down on drug use in the workplace. People were being pissed test randomly, and it also depended on the field of expertise or job sensitivity a person worked. I worked in a local shop, so I was not affected that much by drug rules and regulations. They were not testing in my area.

So here I am, 32 years old, single, and with a good-paying job. I had some money saved up, believe it or not. My use of pot, marijuana, weed, whatever you want to call it, had slowed. In fact, I had quit smoking pot altogether for a while. Believe it or not, I was up for a promotion as a supervisor. I cleaned up my act because I feared getting drug tested.

Three or four years later, I was introduced to a new drug in my life. It was called cocaine. I truly am a victim of my own circumstances. I've always believed that bad things would never happen to me—a good code to live by. Around 1989, things started to really change in my life. I guess I would say I introduced myself to cocaine, not crack cocaine, but don't worry, it was right around the corner, figuratively speaking. I had heard about cocaine. I had seen people snort it. It was known as the rich man's drug; it was pricey. It just didn't make a lot of sense to me to spend money like that for something that only gets you high for about 30 seconds.

"Sucking it up your nose. Oh no, I pass... but not for long. I begin to rationalize it with my sick thinking."It does not stay in your system long compared to pot, which one joint stays in your system for over 30 days. Are you thinking what I am thinking? I could do this cocaine on my day off, and it would be out of my system in about 3 days, four at the most... My stinking thinking.

Sounds like the ideal drug for me. So you know what happened next, that's right, this old boy started snorting cocaine. It was more of a pleasure drug for me. It was more complicated to get a hold of most drug dealers who were into selling pot... Pot was really the drug at the time I was trying to avoid because I still had my eyes on that supervisor promotion; for several years, I was totally drug-free. No pot, no cocaine. I had started back playing softball. But really, this was the quiet before the storm.

In 1986, my mother, the sweet and kind-hearted woman whom God put in my life, passed away. That's when I felt that things in my life started to take a turn for the worse. I moved back out to the country with my father, who was in his late 70s, and he did not want to move to the city, so I moved back to the country with him. I proceeded to fix up the old country house; we began to bond quite well. He was a man of few words, yet very energetic for his age. He was a humble man. He smoked his Prince Albert cigarettes, and yes, he still had his occasional drink; I bought him a car so he could get around in the country. He would go to the post office in Sherrill and visit some of his old friends. That's what really made him happy. He would spend his days tinkering on something, anything to keep him busy. I worked the graveyard shift, and on the weekend, I played softball; some weekends, I got off on Friday mornings and would not show back up until time to go to work on Sunday night. My dad thought I was a professional ball player. I really enjoyed being around him. He was a man of few words, but the few words he spoke carried a lot of worth. I look back now, and I really see how strong he was. To take a child and raise him like your own, and give him love and understanding about the things he knows as a man. He had a 4th-grade education, he knew how to read and write, and he could repair just about anything that was broken. He had a heart of gold to take a child in those times, feed and clothe him while his biological father lived in the same town. My biological father, Charlie Marshall, got me into this world, but Will Harts maintained me in it, and for that, I am forever grateful.

Moving back to the country was really boring. There was no cable TV, no running water, and no indoor toilet. Life was really dull. The little ole town that used to be jumping when I was a kid was no longer there. Most people whom I grew up with had moved away. Sherrill, my hometown, was totally different compared to when I was a kid. Back in the early '50s, it was a jumping town. It had three cotton gins, three grocery stores, a jail, a liquor store, and a sheriff (who owned the liquor store), and no town is complete without a post office. It had two cafes, and on a Saturday night, the cafes would be packed. People really had a good time. Every now and then, a fight would break out—nothing too serious. Both cafes were owned by the same person, Mr. Charlie; Mr Charlie also had a clothing store where he sold second-hand clothing. Sherrill had a booming economy. Cotton was the biggest boost to the town during the '50s. The population back then was about 300 people, which has now dwindled to about 100 people, very few of them I knew.

Things had changed in my life and my surroundings. There was nothing to do that fit my interests. I played a lot of softball. Some of the guys on the team drank beer, smoked pot, and snorted a little cocaine. We would always blaze up before a game. Smoking pot and from time to time snorting a line of cocaine—yes, cocaine— it seemed I could not escape it. I remembered it from my previous experiences. Just imagine smoking pot, drinking beer, snorting cocaine, smoking cigarettes, and getting out ripping and running in the hot, blazing summer sun. I was in my late 30s during this time period.

My dad once told me, and I am sure you have heard the saying yourself, that "God takes care of fools and babies." Well, I am not a baby... moving on. This kind of lifestyle went on for a few years. Even this was getting boring.

Around 1990, I was introduced to something that would completely change my life. An introduction that would send my life spiraling out of control.Slowly but surely. It would destroy my inner ambitions and totally bankrupt my soul, and I would love every minute of it. At least, that's what it made me think. Now let's be honest; I heard about this drug and what it does to people, how it destroys people, ruins lives and families, and the list goes on and on, but like I told myself, this will never happen to me. I am always in control. Wrong!! Oh, how wrong I was. I am sure you have said that at some point in your life." That will never happen to me." Well, it happened to me. Crack cocaine, and I fell for it, hook, line and sinker.

How could something that small have so much power? The more you smoke, the more you want. I remember my first hit. I was not impressed, but I never forgot the taste. They say, One hit, and you are hooked. Well, that worked for me. I am a witness. At the time, I could not see myself paying that kind of money for a high that only lasted about ten seconds. Crack cocaine was not like pot; it was not like snorting cocaine; it had a totally different effect.

I quit smoking pot in 1989 for a period of time. It would be a long time before I would smoke pot again. They say you put down one habit and pick up another; well, I was certainly following the patterns. I gradually started smoking crack cocaine. I became a "one hit will do" smoker, to a "let's do one together" smoker, to an only on payday smoker, to a now and then smoker, to let me hold some until payday smoker. Sound crazy, right? I had become that type of user. In other words, a crackhead, that was me.

My habit, my addiction—whatever you might want to label it—had truly begun to surface. I was spending more money on crack than you can imagine. And my usage was beginning to show. I was doing all the things that I had said I would not do to get it. Lying, cheating, and stealing just to get it. I started missing days from work, showing up late, and more.

My financial world was moving up because I had gotten a promotion on the job, and I was now a supervisor. Now, on the other hand, my moral compass was moving in the opposite direction, down; it's like passing yourself on a glass elevator. You see yourself going up and down at the same time. Sometimes, I would not get any sleep for 48 hours or more. I barely ate—who wants food when you can get high? Sometimes, the mere thought of food would make me sick. This isn't pot; pot gives you the munchies; crack takes it away. That episode went on for a few years. I managed to stay below the radar. I never got piss tested.

I have always been a muscular type of man, weighing over 240 pounds, but with my usage of crack, I had lost down to 195 pounds. Yes, I was looking terrible, and the scars were beginning to show. I was neglecting my personal hygiene. There were times I did not want to look at myself in a mirror. I did not want to face my shame. A great transformation had finally taken over.

The worst experience I had was in June of 1991. It was a Thursday, to the best of my remembrance. I worked third shift at the railroad. I had gotten off that morning, gone home, greeted my dad when I got home, and I went to sleep. I probably sleep for about an hour or so. I wanted to get up and do some early fishing in the pond before it got too hot. The pond was right across the highway. I got up and walked past my dad, sitting in his old recliner, feet all propped up, taking a nap. He had opened a can of peaches and poured them into a bowl, and he had a cigarette lying beside the bowl that had not been lit. I walked past my dad in his recliner, taking a peaceful nap. I went past him into the kitchen to fix myself a bite to eat. I reach under the old cabinet to get a skillet. In doing so, I pulled out several other pans, making a loud noise in the process. I said to myself, I hope I didn't wake my dad with all that noise. I walk to the living room to check on my dad. He was sitting in the same position. I said that it was odd that all that noise did not wake him.

I stood motionless in the doorway; it seemed like, for a minute, I was trying to detect breathing from a distance. He had on an old t-shirt, and the ceiling fan was blowing. It was hard to detect breathing from the distance I was. I slowly moved toward him, my heart pumping and beating fast. My breathing was becoming louder, and every step that I took to get closer to him gave me an uncomfortable feeling. I finally got close enough to touch him. I touched him. He was as cold as ice. He was dead. My dad had died in his sleep. He looked so peaceful. I have always said, "That's the way to go."

I called the Sheriff's Department to report my dad's death. The coroner and the sheriff arrived about 30 minutes later; several people stopped by to see what was going on. The news was traveling fast.

My dad was the church treasurer, and somewhere in this house is the church money. My mind began to focus on where that money could be. Yeah, that's terrible, but I wanted to get high. That's how bad this addiction had gotten. Now you are stealing from God and the church, really? Is this what you are doing, Jimmy? Is this what you have become? "Thou shalt not steal..."

This little episode does not end here. Quickly after the coroner and everyone else had left, I proceeded to search for the money; it didn't take me long to find it. Getting to some crack was now my main course of business. I honestly tell you, it was all I could do to keep from passing the hearse that was carrying my father's body to the funeral home. That's how sick I was. But if the truth be told, which it is, the next 10 years would be the most challenging years of my life. Time went on, and so did my usage of crack cocaine. The reality of my life and circumstances began to creep into my head. I was using more, and life was getting out of control. I was working just to give my money to a drug dealer. Yeah, that's right; now I was dealing directly with the small-time drug dealers. Some of them were people I knew before the crack epidemic began. Some of them worked for the same company that I worked for. And let me make this clear: I never bought crack at the job, nor did I ever use crack on the job. I was trying to distance those activities from my work as best as I could. I would have someone else get my crack, so I would not be seen in certain neighborhoods. Trying to hide what was written all over my face, I found myself sneaking into the neighborhoods that I did not want to get caught in. Oh, how God watches over fools. The craving didn't care about the neighborhood; the craving had to be fed. The fear I had about being in places of danger had become numb. My motto was, "Get in and get out, know who you are dealing with, and never buy from a stranger."

Now, I am living a double life and working at the railroad, trying to stay under the radar; trying to keep my identity hidden from my co-workers... Pretending, hiding, trying to keep up the facade, while all the time I am truly exposed.

I had a co-worker come to my job; his name was Sam. Sam told me about the rumors he had heard and what he knew about me, what was going on in my life, and how I needed to get a grip on my life. He said, "Jimmy, if you don't stop doing what you are doing, you are going to lose it all, including your life." "There are people out there, as well as here on your job, who want to see you fail." He went on to say, "I don't want to see that happen to you; you are a good person. Get yourself some help." Now, Sam came to my job to talk to me on his day off—that's right, his day off. Any railroad worker will tell you that they don't want any part of the railroad on their day off unless they are coming to pick up their paycheck. I am so thankful that Sam did that because that conversation planted a seed. He and I are friends today, and every now and then, I will visit him. He will tell you that I don't let him forget how thankful I am for what he did.

The year was the fall of 1991. My sister and a friend intervened and got me into Rehab. I did not want any part of that, even though I really needed help. I was mad because my so-called secret was out. I had in my insane crack world mind that nobody was gonna stop me from smoking crack. I didn't want any intervention by anyone. I cussed and raised hell all the way to rehab, which was about an hour or so away. I attempted to jump out of a moving car. Stupid, stupid, stupid. But my sister, thank God, was persistent. She settled me down and got me all checked into rehab.

I spent 45 days in the rehab center. Not wanting to be there did not help. I felt embarrassed more than anything else I could think of. The fear of losing my job for the first time really began to set in. I felt really worthless to myself. I experienced some of the worst lows in life that I had ever felt.

For the first 24 hours, all I did was sleep. That was something I really had not done in the past. I was working and smoking the hell out of crack—no rest. I spent those 45 days there reluctantly, not really getting into the program that was being offered. I was being introduced to a different side of the drug, crack cocaine: the "how to keep yourself from using" side. It introduced me to how to deal with people, places, and things, as well as how to cope with life on life's terms. I didn't know I had a problem; I thought I just liked to get high. I really didn't know that getting high was going to be such a problem. Oh, how I was in denial. I thought only drug addicts and alcoholics went to rehab. I had a very bad case of denial. I am not a drug addict or an alcoholic.

Why am I here? I tried convincing myself that I was not an addict, so why am I here? Anyone who has been to a rehab center can relate to this. You don't want to hear what the counselors are trying to tell you about recovery. In fact, your mind is off in La La Land, thinking about what you will do when you get out, and what you want to do has nothing to do with the program. I completed my 45 days in the program. It was more of a job saver than anything else. Did I get anything out of the program? Yes and no.

Let's start with the "no" aspect. Truthfully speaking, I really did not apply myself to achieve anything useful, even though the rehab program was presented to me in a very helpful manner. I was not focused. I had a different thought process that was going to lead me right back to the program. Where are my friends, places, and things? I did not want to deal with any kind of logic. It's hard to see in the darkness with no light; the light is there, but you have to pull the switch yourself. As for me, I was not ready to pull that switch. I finished the program. I had a few months of clarity and sobriety—more clarity than sobriety—then I relapsed. The one word I heard over and over and remember from rehab was the word "relapse." The one word that all the counselors stressed and talked about was "relapse." What they said was the truth, not that I doubted them to begin with. I was just not receptive to what they were saying. It's obvious my way of thinking and doing got me to Rehab, and my way of thinking and doing was going to bring me back.

The Letter

Today was my seven-year anniversary with my wonderful husband. As always, he was very good to me. He cooked a very special dinner for me. It was great; the table setting was impressive. That's my Jim, he is always perfect in everything he does. He takes a lot of pride. I am grateful to him and my family, even in the imperfections of some of my children. They are still the love of my life. I am grateful to be their mom and have them in my life. And for Seth, who is so responsible and caring and not selfish and not self-centered. I feel Seth will always affect people in a positive way. I am also grateful for my husband, who sometimes has gotten the short end of the stick. I hope someday to be able to return that to him. I am grateful for my man, grandson. He brings me so much joy. He is beautiful, so very smart, and makes me laugh daily. I love you, Drake, so very much, and I know you love me. I love to hear you say, Nannie or Nan. I love to hear you say Paw Paw. Your love and devotion are so genuine. I am grateful for having you as my grandchild. I hope my family knows how much I love them. I have a wonderful sister. I am grateful for her and the relationship that we have. Justin, you are a good-looking man, and it is so hard to believe you are nineteen years old; it brings tears to my eyes, and I don't know why. I guess it's because I worry about you so much. I would die if anything were to happen to you or Peyton. We have a special bond that I never want to let go of. I pray to God to take care of you. I am glad and grateful for seven years of marriage to my wonderful husband.

The letter you just read was written on March 11, 1999, our wedding date seven years prior. In 1992, I met and married Brenda, and I made changes in my life. I felt a sense of purpose. I mentioned my issues to her concerning my drug usage and how I was trying to put my past behind me and move forward. We had good and bad years, ups and downs. But we weathered the storms together. I was still slipping and falling, but I always got myself up. I was not falling as much, but to be honest, I was still falling. In the words of Michael Jackson, "I started looking at that man in the mirror. I made all the decisions in my life; it's obvious I have been making some bad decisions. I mean, I really had to take an inventory of my life. Now more than ever, I am married, have children, have a family, and have more responsibility. The decisions I make affect other people. Up until now, I have been escaping with this drug thing only by the grace of the Creator. These are some of the things you must accept. The key word is accept before you can proceed forward. I accepted the fact that I am an addict because my actions up to this point in life have proven this to be true. I accepted the fact that I was in denial because my actions up to that point proved that to be true. I accepted the fact that I needed help because my actions in my life showed that I do.

When I think of my life, certain words come to mind...

Utah. That's right, Utah. What's in Utah? Choices, options and destiny. I have made some bad choices, which are now leading to my options, that have led me to an unknown destiny. I am headed to a place called Highland Ridge. Yes, Highland Ridge is a rehab center where the Railroad sends its employees who have substance abuse problems. I fit that profile.

The next 21 days more or less deal with my stay at this facility, how this facility really impacted my life, and, in some ways, shaped my future.

This is my third 3rd stint in rehab. The 3rd time is a charm.. Right? Or is it 3 strikes you're out? Anyway, I am here, and I am here by my own choice. There is something about going to rehab this time that I really feel different about. You hear people say that if you are tired of doing the same destructive things and making the same mistakes over and over, you should change what you are doing. You should change your game plan.

I am not going reluctantly; this time, I am going willingly and with an open mind. I hope to stop the vicious circle my life is going through. I am no longer in denial. I have a very serious problem, and my life has become unmanageable. Maybe this is my destiny.

The airplane landed in St. Louis; it was nightfall. I will be in St. Louis for a short time for a flight change.

I remember having that feeling of being all alone. But for now, I am just glad to have my feet back on solid ground. Never had I really flown that much, and the few times I did, I did not like it. So here I am, with no money, nothing but hope. Hope—maybe sometimes that's all a person needs.

I really wish I could turn off the replay in my head concerning the last couple of weeks. In the past couple of weeks, we've nearly reached four thousand dollars. We just received our income tax return. We were essentially trying to recover from the Christmas holidays and catch up on bills. As always, I paid a majority of the bills; let's be honest, I paid all the bills. Paying the bills gave me a feeling of real responsibility, and I could also keep up with how much I could sneak and spend on crack. I knew that I could not be trusted with money, especially since, in the last three or four months, I was out again sneaking and buying crack. But I kept telling myself that I had this under control. My usage was getting back to the point it had been before I was married; that was not good. I knew what the outcome was going to be every time I sneaked, and when Brenda was working, there were times I would be late picking her up, and I would try to defend myself in the process. There was no excuse for my action, but there was a reason... Crack.

I knew what the outcome was going to be when I smoked crack. I could tell my own future every time; the results were always the same. I ignored the warnings, and by now, I am too deep into my convictions. I am at the airport, hungry, and can't buy a hamburger. I want to feel sorry for myself, but I can't; there's no time for pity because I am too busy feeling like a fool.

It's 6:25 in St. Louis; the next stop is Utah. As I stared out the window, watching planes land and take off, a great sadness came over me concerning Brenda. Leaving her behind to deal with my fallout really hurt. I know this is a mental drain on her, and for that, I am sorry and hope she finds ways to forgive me once she gets an understanding of how addiction works.

It's 10:15 p.m. I have arrived at the airport in Utah. I got to meet up with this man named Pete; he is my pick-up guy, and he was my ride to the treatment center. I talked with Pete on the phone before I left home. Pete said he would meet me in the middle of the world... Okay.

I departed the plane and worked my way to the airport lobby. There was this man standing in the middle of the floor; I didn't pay much attention until I glanced down at his feet. Believe it or not, he was standing in the middle of the world. I don't recall what airport this is, but on the floor is a map of the world; he was standing right in the middle of the world. I kind of laughed as I walked up to him and introduced myself. Pete let out a sigh. "That gets them every time," he said.

As we left the airport, Pete began to talk. I was not in a talking mood, but I listened as my mind continued to wander while I looked out the car window.

Pete begins to tell me some of his war stories. I hate war stories, but as Pete began to talk, a calmness came over me. War stories are stories about your use, whether you are an addict, alcoholic, etc. It seems some people seem to glorify their stories and exploits. I am trying to forget them; they cause pain. After hearing Pete say he was an addict, I began to open up and talk a little more. Pete was an addict who had been clean and sober for 12 years. In my opinion, it's much easier to converse with someone who has similar issues.

We pulled into Highland Ridge. I got out and shut the

door, and Pete reached over, shook my hand, and wished me luck. It would be 21 days before I would see Pete again. I remember telling myself I was missing no one and that no one was missing me. Welcome to Utah.

21 Days

As I walked down the halls of Highland Ridge, I closed my eyes for a moment. It reminded me of Charter Hospital, where I was in 1991. Now, ten years later, I am still working on myself. I continued through the swinging doors to the nurse's station, and to my right, another set of swinging doors led to a different room. In that room, I see nothing but faces. To me, those faces represent choices—some chose to be here, others are court-ordered, and some feel it's their destiny. Somewhere in this web, I find my place.

No PlayStation 2, no DVD, no HBO, no little dogs barking, I will miss them, no going to the fridge to get a midnight snack, no going to my game room to shoot pool at home. It is very clear I am not home. I know the boredom will set in, but I am determined to get my life back on track. Tonight, I sleep with strangers, strangers with whom I have a lot in common. It took about an hour or so for me to get settled in. I was familiar with the check-in process and all the questions they asked. This was not my first rodeo. I was hungry, but I arrived here too late to eat; they did allow me to get some snacks from the commissary.

Had my first night of sleep; they put me in a room with a guy named Steve. Now, this guy had a sleeping problem. He snored all night long; I mean all night. I never heard anyone snore like Steve in my life. I was thinking, "Lord, don't let this guy be my roommate. Because if he is, I've got a problem; I don't want a problem." I managed to get some sleep. I recall having a very pleasant dream—a dream about my mother, the one who raised me. It was one of the most pleasant dreams I had had in a while. I dreamed I was back home in my hometown of Sherrill, Arkansas. She was cleaning the house. Maybe this dream was telling me that if I cleaned up my life, everything would be okay.

Day one... It's 6:20 am, Feb 8, 2003, and I just had my blood work done. I suffer from high blood pressure. Being black and smoking crack and having high blood pressure, you are really playing with your life. My blood pressure was somewhat high, probably because Steve snored all night.

"Come to find out, Steve was a mental patient... What?"

Steve was a psycho; according to one of the daytime nurses, we were not supposed to be in the same room. Now, I am really scared. Y'all put me in a room with a crazy person. As I began to settle in, my mind was dwelling on what Brenda had said before I left to come to Utah. We had a big argument on the way to the airport. She called me a weak person, a "pussy." She said I was running away from problems instead of facing them. I felt some truth in that, and it hurt. I also felt that every time I faced my issues with crack, I lost. It was time to do something different and meaningful. There are a lot of things I know, and there are some things that I will not accept. I will not accept my life continuing to go this way. I know better, I can do better, and I will do better. I know my life is out of control, and right now, it is very unmanageable. I believe I will get out of the program what I put into it. I am just surviving, not living. I want to live. I believe that by being here and applying myself, in return, I give myself a chance to live. But Brenda did not have any of that, and I understood.

Day 2... Yesterday was full of formalities. I basically did nothing yesterday but get settled in. Now, everyone knows that to start your day off, you need a good breakfast. I don't think the people here at the Treatment Facility read that message. The food sucked, let's be honest. Everyone was complaining about the food. I came into the program to get cleaned up and hopefully lose a pound or two. It has been said that most people gain weight when they go to a treatment center. You are eating healthy food, getting rest, and you are drug-free. I was not the only one complaining.

All in all, it was a good day. I was the new kid on the block, all eyes on me. I met others who worked for the railroad, which made things a bit easier. I was in my late forties; I think the oldest railroad worker was 61 years old. There were some non-railroad workers as young as 17 years old. The feeling of embarrassment that I had was beginning to ease a bit. Talking to people with common problems and issues let me know I was not alone.

I did not like the wire fences; they made me feel like a caged animal, a prisoner. There were some who paced back and forth like animals in a cage. Come to find out, they were on medication. Underneath it all, I was a prisoner of my addiction, a slave to the insanity of crack cocaine.

Today, I spoke in the group, mainly about my time at Charter Hospital. Highland Ridge was different. This place is busy; you are doing something constructive basically all day. I saw the doctor that I was assigned to. He said everything health-wise was okay; blood pressure was high as usual. You really tear yourself down when you are drugging, not eating properly, not getting rest, and having days without sleep. Especially when I was single, it was unbelievable what I put my body through: poor personal hygiene. What they call binges can be killers. A binge is when you go for several days without eating. All you are doing is smoking and smoking and smoking.

I got my own room today. I was placed on the side where the addicts were. No more 'Steve the snorer." Maybe tonight I'll get some good sleep.

I have only been here two days, and I have an assignment. I've got to write a brief auto on how I think my drug use may have started. That's going to be a trip, I said to myself.

Bedtime around here is 10 p.m., and looking at my watch, it's about that time. I am not much into praying, even though I was raised in a household where church was part of our life. My mother made sure I went to church; in fact, I was baptized and was also a member of Corinth Missionary Baptist. As I lay in bed, feeling empty and wondering what Brenda was doing back home, I knew this was not something I should be thinking about. Besides, there is nothing I can do here that's going to help my situation back home at the moment. I have to stay focused, but I do miss home. God, I know you are watching down on me; you know my every move. I am asking that you protect my family. I am asking that you have mercy on me. Help me with my weakness; give me strength to overcome. Wash away my stupidity and help me with my recovery. You are all I need; I know and believe this. I want to live.

Day 3... I am beginning to feel more at ease. I have gotten acquainted with most people in my group. I feel comfortable in my setting. What will I talk about today? It's time for breakfast, and most of us gather in what is called the community room. We have to go eat at certain times. Because there are other patients, some are mental, and some are children with issues. As I sat waiting for my group to go eat, I heard this playing on the radio by Eric Clapton entitled Cocaine. How quaint. That should get my day rolling, I thought to myself.

Rehab, to me, is like a hit of cocaine. After that first hit, everything becomes repetitive, but this is what we addicts must go through if we want to recover. I could not grasp this concept when I was in rehab before. Here is another thing I could grasp: the first hit you take of crack is the highest you are going to get. You are like a dog that chases its tail; you are not going to get any higher. No matter how much time or money you spend, you are not going to get any higher. A ten-second euphoric high is what you get. After that, all you are buying is misery, but we, as crack addicts, seem to love it.

I will admit that if not for the consequences, I would probably still be using, well, maybe not; I would probably be dead, like a lot of users who died in their addictions. I would be no different than the person who is overweight, who loves to eat, but eating is bad for your health as well as your lifestyle. I think you get the picture. Otherwise, my day 3 went pretty smoothly.

Day 4... Things are beginning to lighten up even more; it seems the less I worry about back home, the more at home I feel in here. After all, I am with a group of people with similar issues. Some people don't want to be here, understandable; some have been court-ordered, forced to be here or go to jail.... Options. Some are here to save their job and marriage, and some are here to save their life.... that's me again. Whatever reason we are here for, we are hoping to make the best of it. Let's face it: sooner or later, that jail thing, including death, was going to catch up to me. Yes, I believed that. I really don't know how other addicts really feel, but I am glad to be here. You get out what you put in. No time for negativism.

Eating breakfast here at Highland Ridge is really the highlight of every morning, but hey, I am ok with that.

There is really a nice view from the eating area of the snow-capped mountains of Utah. You can always see the snow as it comes down from the mountains. It's like a slow-moving fog. It's February, and they are having what's called snow showers. It's like rain showers, but it's snow. You see them coming from a distance.

One of the main issues today was that one of the group members was dismissed because of his attitude. It was a very touchy situation. It got a little heated. I thought the guy was a little intimidating. He did not get along with other people too well. He was really a bully. He only picked on people he figured he could intimidate or people who were smaller in size than he was, including one of the counselors. Come to find out, later on, this guy was sent from jail; he was court-ordered.

Somehow, I got caught up in the situation because I more or less took up for another person. I was just trying to be a peacemaker. I was called in to speak to the head counselor. I gave my opinion on the situation. This guy had just about interrupted the whole day. He was very disruptive to the community. The question was, should he be dismissed? I gave my opinion; yes, he should be dismissed. It was obvious he did not want to be here. He had gotten into a fight, which was the reason he was in jail. He had scars on his face and hands to prove it. They dismissed the guy for obvious reasons. There were mixed emotions.

But all in all, most wanted him gone. Some people felt they did not need to be in the program. He was one of the ones who felt that way. There were others, but they were not disruptive. I felt that way at my first intervention and rehab. I was not ready to quit. Therefore, I did not apply myself. I was in total denial.

Day 5... Yes, breakfast was lousy, but it's getting better. Some people will be leaving this weekend. As we put it, they have served their time. I have been voted community leader of our group; I didn't see that coming. Everyone here is great people, especially the staff, who always work with a smile.

Paul, one of the guys in the group, got some sad news today. His wife called to tell him that she had filed for divorce. That's not the kind of news you want to hear when you are in a place like this. Most of the guys thought this was a dirty blow since the guy was trying to get his life together. It really made me think about my situation back home because I did not leave on the best of terms, but that's part of the fallout. The group wished him the best. I feel for Paul, but his wife has a side of the story, also. I was in the program today, and I had to discuss my anger. My anger dealt with my life. The fact that my life was spiraling out of control was my fault. My ship was sinking and I was taking other people with me, my family. Sometimes, with me, this addict concept is hard to accept. Brenda said I was selfish and not considerate of others. I disagree, but everyone has a right to their opinion.

As I sat in the group today, I noticed one of the young

ladies crying; she had just finished her bio. She was asked by the counselor Why are you crying? What's wrong? She responded by saying how screwed up her life had become. As I said, she had just finished her bio, which left everyone in a state of awe. Her life at such a young age was quite a story. She was living a fast life filled with drugs and sex. She was a dancer, free-spirited, I would assume, a really talented person. For a while in her life, I would say she had it going on. Today we all had to go to an A A meeting; It was a first. I listen to other people tell their stories and how they are progressing in life. These people were out of the program and going to meetings, which was part of the healing process. My day will come.

Day 6... Sweetheart day. Happy Valentine's Day! Brenda got an opportunity to talk with her for a brief moment. I had no apologies to offer; I hoped she was doing ok. I finished my bio last night; I am eager to present it, but all in due time. I was appointed community group leader yesterday. It was a good feeling to know that in the short time I had been here, I had gained trust because I had lost it back home. I had said I was so sorry so many times in the past. It's a word I try to keep out of my vocabulary, even today. Brenda was tired of hearing it anyway, and I was tired of lying. In here, I am being honest with myself and the people around me. My goal while I am here is to do the things I should have done in my previous rehabs.

I see the writing on the wall. There are no tomorrows for me if I don't get this right today. I feel positive about my life. Maybe one day I can come back and give my success story. They had a guy named Troy come in a couple of days ago and give his story. It really left me with a positive attitude. He really started all over and rebuilt his life. He said it was an everyday journey for him. But now I must work on the obstacles ahead of me; I admit I am fearful, very fearful. But I will face these once I get over all the embarrassment. I hate failing. I always thought I could beat the drug thing, but so far, it has bested me, but I am headed in the right direction. The real failures are still out there using. The first step to recovery is to admit you have a problem. That's simple, right? That's harder than one would think. Admitting failure.

Since I have been here, several people have checked in. One was put out, and three checked in today. The ones who get checked in all have that I don't want to be here look. Welcome. We will be having closing ceremonies this evening for the ones who will be leaving. I kind of hate to see them go, even though we just met a couple of days ago. I wish when I go, I could bottle this feeling and atmosphere and take it with me, but it just doesn't work that way. But you can take it with you if you apply yourself. I know once they get out of this protected environment, the real test begins. In my first rehab, I made it probably a week, then I was back to my old tricks, right where the crack wanted me. I say to myself, Lord, don't let me fail, but that responsibility is mine. I have to take it upon myself. This is an I gotta do thing, not God gotta do.

This is the first time in about 20 years that I am drug-free, alcohol-free, and nicotine-free. Yes, I quit smoking cigarettes as well. Smoking cigarettes and lighting them up reminded me of lighting up a crack pipe. On this day, February 14, 2003, I am drug-free.

Today is day 7... My first week here at Highland Ridge. I got 17 days of clean time, counting the 10 days before I arrived here. It's a slow climb, but I plan to get there; today is family day. I don't expect any family to show up. I am a long way from home. To me, that's a good thing. I don't need any distraction; I would like to feel that I have crossed Brenda's mind in a nice way. I have earned a ground pass. A ground pass allows you to leave the premises. Well, I just got a pass because I am going nowhere; we all have to go to family day, whether we have family or not.

One of the younger guys in the group, Cory's family, was here. They had Cory and his father in a one-on-one setting, and we, as a group, had to observe and ask questions if we wanted to. To me, the most moving statement was from Cory himself. Cory stated he had learned a lot by coming to the family meetings. Cory said that he had learned by coming to the meeting that his addiction was a disease and a sickness. I know some people feel that way, and some feel the opposite. I often wonder about that statement. But what do I know? Once you experience something good or bad, you have a tendency never to forget the experience. Like riding a bike, you don't forget even the times you fell off. How do you eliminate that from your mind? Getting high with crack cocaine was what I liked, but I was really overjoyed at the fact that Cory's dad was taking an interest in his son's recovery.

In recovery, you really need family support. That is one of the reasons you are put in a group. After the family meeting, the rest of the day was really free time. I took the time to work on my steps. After all, this is a 12-step program. Another guy named Trent would eventually become my roommate. We walked around the compound. The mountains that surrounded the compound were spellbinding. I found myself just staring at the snowy mountains. Some mountains seem to have a beckoning call... Come to climb me... No, I pass. But Midvale, Utah, is a lovely place.

Day 8... Same morning routine, breakfast, medication, meditation, and so on. My roommate Trent and I went for a walk. We left the compound, but we found out later that leaving the compound was a no-no. Well, here I go, breaking the rules. Fortunately, we did not get in trouble, mainly because no one caught us. It was nice for Trent and me to walk, talk, and reflect. We will be having another closing ceremony for one of the patients who will be leaving today. We went to an open N A meeting that evening. Trent read his step 3 to me. It was quite touching. We talked quite a bit about our addiction and the similarities. Trent did pills.

I did crack, but we ended up in the same treatment facility. I really loved talking with Trent. We bonded quite well. God, I hope he makes it. He has a loving family, judging from his conversation. His family did come down to see him yesterday for family day. His family drove over three hundred miles to be here, which I am sure made him feel proud. I talked with Brenda today, and judging from her voice, she seems ok. I heard something in an NA meeting that I must share... Religion is what people practice to keep from going to hell. Spiritually, it is what they practice when they have been through hell.

Day 9... A lot went on today, besides the regular routine. Some people were changing living quarters, nobody checked out, and nobody checked in, but it was still a frightening day. Two people went to the hospital..Jeff, one of the patients who checked in over the weekend, really gave us a scare. I really thought the poor guy was dying. He was having a seizure. As he fell, his head hit a concrete ledge in the outdoor smoking area. It created a cut on his forehead. I mean, he fell like a ton of bricks. I was the first to reach him, as his eyes were rolling back in his head. I really thought Jeff was dying.

All of a sudden, his body went limp. I said to myself, this man is dead. The ambulance arrived and carried him to the hospital. Another patient was freaking out over meds. She was very disruptive. Later on that day, Jeff returned to the treatment center with his head all bandaged. He was released the next day due to his medical condition. I had bad emotional feelings today, and panic mode set in. All of a sudden, the fear of my addiction came over me. I realize this recovery thing is really serious. Being in here is just the beginning. There is so much to do once I get out; I can't stay here forever. I think it is called anxiety. I think about the people I have to face. My job is rebuilding trust with fellow employees and my family, getting into a program, going to meetings, and, oh yeah, finding a sponsor. I am going to have to go through my personal inventory and have a life cleansing, get rid of the unusable, the meaningless, and the useless. Really changed my way of thinking. All of a sudden, I feel like I am having a panic attack. Tara, who was part of the group, checked herself out today. I do not think anyone will miss her. She did not seem to take the program seriously, and I understood that she was not ready to come in from madness. I have been there, and she will be back. I hope. Trust me, she will be back.

Day 10... I have 11 days to go, not that I am counting them down, but I am counting them up. Breakfast was good...Whoa!!! Did I say breakfast was good? Yes, I did, and so was lunch. Today is a special day for me. I get a one-on-one with my counselor, and today I will present my auto. I am ready for it. Circumstances will get better in my life. I have faith it will... I called one of my bosses (Roger) and thanked him for getting me into the program... I thanked him for being concerned. Sometimes, we just want someone to show they care. He could have really ended my career. Thanks, Roger.

I hear today they are going to move me over to the apartments later this week. The apartment move is part of the program process. I have been reading my Bible lately at night, Psalms 23. I admit I have not been one for reading the Bible much, but that has not dampened my belief in God. As an only child, my parents made sure I went to church. Was I getting anything out of it? That's another yes and no answer. As a child, it was a place to go and play with other kids. But it helped me during my upbringing as a young man. My understanding of going now is clear. Even though my mind is clouded with questions, we will leave this topic for another day. In the program, they say *Let go and let God.* Some things are hard to let go of. God didn't get me into this mess; I did, so why would God get me out of it? Hell, I knew better. I thank God for being there, protecting me while I tried to self-destruct. This goes back to babies and fools. Like I said earlier, I ain't no baby, so I must be a... Well, you get the picture. But if we are to recover, we must turn our will over to the loving God as we know him to be. In the group, I found some had a hard time dealing with that concept. In fact, some would go as far as to blame God. In group sessions, I sit and listen to them struggle with step 3; some would go as far as to blame God for their struggles. These were some of the things my roommate and I would discuss. He and I would talk about certain things in the Bible. He would give me his beliefs and thoughts, and in return, I would give mine. I believe Trent was a Mormon. He talked about the Book of

Mormon, and I had no concept of what he was talking about. I quickly became a listener; I know what that is. Some of the things he mentioned were simply amazing. We talked about prejudice in America. He said he did not understand why there was so much prejudice. Trent was 38 years old. This was the first time he had spent the night in a room with a black man.

Trent was raised in Kanab, Utah. He went on to tell me a lot of Westerns were filmed in Utah, as well as the Planet of the Apes with Charlton Heston. I was amazed by all of this. We talked about our addiction and what it had done to our families, and how sad it made us feel. Trent and I formed a pack. That pack was within 30 minutes of getting out of the treatment center; we would send each other a postcard to let the other person know we were doing okay. If one of us did not respond, that meant one of us had relapsed.

Day 11... I am still counting my days down. Breakfast is tasting better every day. Maybe when I arrived here, I had bad taste in my mouth, I don't know. Today was a slack day. I finally got around to reading my auto. It was good to get that off my chest. Enjoyed the men's session today. Somehow, this reminded me of being back at school. I wish I were. The afternoon was more recreation than anything. We played volleyball, shot some hoops, and played some card games. I've got to get some exercise into my program. Each day here, I feel stronger about myself; each day, I learn more about my addiction and how to cope with it on a recovery basis. The drug is stronger, but I feel I am smarter. This program is giving me the tools to overcome it. These are tools I can and must use for my recovery. I do not want to get caught up in some kind of I am going to change the world campaign, but someday, I truly hope I can give back, but I leave all that to God. God knows what's best for me. I pray I get myself in the right frame of mind to face the things ahead. Even though I have been tossing the question around in my head about how to handle my situation once I am back home, I am sure lies have been told, rumors have been spread, and I am sure of that. Will I be straight up, or will I be evasive? Will I let the truth be told from my lips or let the rumors circulate from their lips? All this could be a trigger. It all depends on how I handle it.

Day 12... 3 guys will be leaving today. Jon, Dennis and Jeff. Jon, the co-leader, was the first person I met as far as the introduction was concerned. I thought Jon was a counselor. Jon was a railroad worker like me, except he was an engineer. We had a great conversation about the railroad. Jon, it seems, had the mentality to succeed; I wished him well, and we promised each other to stay in contact. The dinner here was great today; I guess it's about attitude. The better your attitude, the better the food tastes. I had a conversation with one of the cooks. I was complimenting her on the food.

We were basically having a general conversation. I told her I was from Arkansas. She stated she was from the Philippines and that she was adopted, and how she got to America. That saying is true; everybody has a story... Today, I moved to the apartments. I will have my own separate room. Three people already live there. When you move to the apartments, that usually means you don't have long to stay in the program. It's a new beginning for me. I got a pass that allowed me to leave the compound. Some of us have planned a visit to downtown Salt Lake City, Utah. It's only about 12 miles from Midvale, Utah, where the treatment center is located.

I will be sightseeing because I really don't have any money. Today was the first time I saw the group so intense. One of the guys in the group felt he was not an addict because his medication was medically prescribed. He really felt he had no problem, but he had prescriptions from doctors all over Utah, really... His medication was OxyContin. Never heard of it until now. But listening to other people talk about OxyContin, it was not anything to mess with. I was not into pill popping. I don't like taking my prescribed meds. If I can't smoke or snort it, I don't want it.

OxyContin, as they called it, is highly addictive. People have been known to overdose on it. I learn something every day. This guy had a high-profile job, a nice fancy car with all the perks; I guess this made him feel invincible. In fact, he drove himself to rehab. Everyone else thought otherwise. Hey, people, addictions don't discriminate. This guy felt he did not need the program. He really felt he was better than us. He said he was just there to detox. He said he could quit at any time. Yeah right... Have you ever just sat and observed people, wondering what really makes them tick? You know, some people have stereotyped addicts; some have only seen them portrayed on television, teeth dirty, clothes all dirty, and hair not combed, but that's not always the case. I look at Rich, another guy in the program. A good job and an easy-going type of person. You would never think, by just looking at Rich, that he has a problem. Rich seems to have suicidal tendencies, but that's just my opinion. He stated he feels worthless; he always feels down on himself. Well, this is what I gather from our conversation. Ron, another railroad worker, just got caught up in the system. Ron states he only drinks sociably; he said he has only been drunk once in his life, one time.

The guy has the background of a priest: another railroad worker, a brother like myself, Earnest. Earnest was a good ole country boy from Texas who thought smoking pot was no big deal; I feel the same way, Earnest. Earnest was amazed at the crack cocaine stories, meth, OxyContin and a few other pain medications that were being abused. This was his 1ˢᵗ time in a rehab program. I bet my life on it. When he gets out, he won't be back. It seems all of us here at Highland Ridge used drugs or alcohol to block out or dull the pain of issues in our lives. I admit I did it on several occasions, but it only made matters worse.

Day 13... I have about one week to go in the program. I am starting to get a little ome sick. I talked with my wife, Brenda, today. She is holding on the best she can under the circumstances. She is a strong woman mentally, I feel blessed to have her in my life, and I love her with all my heart. I know this has been an ordeal for her. Brenda went on to tell me she was concerned about Jonathan. Jonathan is her oldest child; She didn't want him drinking and driving because in the past it had led to bad things. I quickly told her that there was nothing I could do about it. I am here, and I can talk with him if she wants me to. He is a grown man who has to own up to his responsibilities.

Brenda was always trying to solve her children's issues, whether they were big or small; she didn't back down. She would tackle them. I didn't always agree with her methods, since they were men. I figured it was time for a little tough love and to let them grow up, but she did not have any of that. Brenda had four children when she and I got married. We have none together. I can truly say that I have never had any issues with any of her children, even in some of my darkest hours. They have always treated me with respect and dignity. She was always looking out for their best interest, and they knew that. I told her that I only had about a week to go, and I felt the program was very helpful to me. She didn't give me too much of a comment back, and that was understandable, very understandable. I talked with my counselor about the situation back home. He stated to me that I must try to understand her feelings. You are here getting help. She is getting none. You left a burden on her to carry on while you are seeking help. In what way do you expect her to feel? How do you expect her to act?

Quit thinking about yourself so much. She is a human being, and she needs counseling as well as you. He stated that he hoped I would work on a co-counseling program once I returned home. The rest of the day was more counseling. A few more bios were presented. The men had their group session. I know I am here because of my past actions. But I am so glad to be here so that my mind might be free of the routine of using and feeling guilty about it. All of this is work within itself. My mind and body needed some healing. My spirit needed an awakening.

Day 14... One of the group members, Jon, will be leaving today. As we sat and ate breakfast, we gave him a group talk and wished him well on his return home and his transition back to work. Jon has been an inspiration to all of us. I wish him the best. Sitting here this morning listening to the morning weather, the weatherman stated there is snow in the forecast coming in the next 5 to 6 days. I understand that some bad weather is expected back home, well, that is not good news for me because I will be leaving in about a week. I really don't want to get snowed in in Utah. It seems it has snowed every day I have been here, nothing overwhelming to cause panic. Bowling is the plan for tomorrow. I hope to get a chance to go, depending on the weather. Bad weather is expected back home as well. The group and the counselor focused on Brenda and my son's situation back home. They said I need to set my boundaries; dealing with this could have a triggering effect once I am home.

I don't consider them to be triggers, but maybe they are. We had our routine group session this morning, and all went well. It seems a lot of the drama we had earlier when I arrived has subsided. I had a fun time in recreation today. We played volleyball and basketball, did a little weight lifting, and walked around the compound. I felt like a kid again. I wish I were... not really, I just wish I could dump all my responsibilities, but part of recovery is being a responsible person. We have to learn to deal with life on life's terms. I look back on my situations where I really screwed up and really saw how irresponsible I was as a person on the job and at home. Only thinking of Jimmy, and even after it was over, I wanted all the pity. I think that angered my wife a lot. She wanted something to hit me and give me a jolt, something that would shock me back to reality and give me a true wake-up call.

Day 15... Debbie or Deb is what she likes to be called. Deb gave her the auto today. She cried the whole time she was reading it. I believe she used a box of tissues to wipe her face as she read; you could also see the relief on her face once she finished. A lot of us, I am sure, felt compassion and sadness in our hearts. We know the after-effects of using drugs or alcohol. You get on that pity pot with yourself. This only happens after, not before. Deb and I came to the treatment center about the same time, and for her, it took courage to tell her story. It being the weekend, we as a group had to sit in on a family session day. To be honest, I had my mind set on back home; I was just going through the motions. Rehab can have a numbing effect. I had my mind set on bowling and things back home about Brenda and the little dogs, grandkids, and the bad weather coming her way. Just seeing the place now would be a welcome relief. I've got to stay focused, with less than a week to go and new challenges ahead, and I get jittery thinking about them. I know the bottom line is I must change my way of thinking, start believing in myself, develop a program to do the 12 steps, and get a sponsor. I will start with the Church and go from there. I believe with all my heart I will make it. It won't be easy, but with God's grace and mercy, I will make it.

Day 16... Still counting them down, today I became a short-timer. This means I don't have long to go; a feeling of anticipation rushes through my body. I am sure you know that feeling, whether you are an addict or not.

Today was an adventurous day. A group of us, about 8. Mike J, Mike C. Ben, Earnest, my brother from Texas, I call him my brother because he is a black guy. I was all alone until Earnest came alone (humor). Deb and Susan came along. Susan was from Utah. We caught the rail train to downtown Salt Lake City, Utah. I didn't like sitting backward on the rail train. I like to see where I am going, not where I have been. It felt awkward. We went downtown and did a little window shopping. I only had about 20 dollars, so I had to be thrifty. We took a tour of downtown Salt Lake City. Mike C lived there, so he was more or less our guide. He gave us a pretty good tour of the city. Downtown Salt Lake City is a beautiful place; I got to see the statue of Brigham Young. I had heard of BYU but did not know it was Utah...silly me. We made it to the Temple Gate but did not venture in. We did quite a bit of walking, and I felt like a kid on a field trip.

Went to the site of the Church of the Latter Day Saints, but we did not enter.

I was overly amazed at the structure of the building; it left me speechless. They say you should not repeat what you hear; know your facts. Is it true there are more Mormons in Utah than anywhere else in the United States? In Utah, Mormons stand for money and power, or is that power and money? Sounds like an oxymoron. There were several people at this Rehab Facility who were Mormons, and their churches were paying for their treatment... Do Christian churches do that?? There is a book called the Book of Mormon. Mike C. said that if you have ever been baptized in the Mormon Faith and it's documented, your name is written in the book of

Mormons... Don't repeat what you just read... moving on.

Salt Lake City, Utah, streets were very, very clean. I saw a lot of mixed Native Americans. There were Latinos and very few blacks. Now, this is not to say Black people don't dwell here. I personally never dreamed I would be in Utah for any reason, especially the reason I am here now. I got a chance to see the Delta Center; that's where Carl (The Mailman) Malone makes his deliveries for the Utah Jazz. Right across from the Delta Center is the Union Pacific Railroad Building. It is all laid out with the big Union Pacific logo on the front and the Union Pacific colors, which are cobalt, red, yellow, and gray. If you are a railroad worker or a past worker and reading this, you are going to fact-check me. Now, when you pass through the Union Pacific building, you come out two stories up inside a Mall (2002), an outdoor Mall with a very scenic view, amazing. I thank God for allowing me to visit such a place.

Maybe one day in the future, I can bring my family

back to visit this place. I had a very good time with the group. We caught the rail train back to the Rehab Center. I was really exhausted and hungry, but as I sat there, this time facing forward. Watching scenery flash by my window. I began to think about my sobriety, which began to bring the thoughts of fear into my head. I do understand that I don't have to do this alone. There are steps I must take. 12 of them are correct. There are things I must have the courage to do to keep myself out of bad situations. Think before you react. See the thought all the way through and ask yourself what result is best for your life. A person must be selfish at this point because it's their life or their livelihood at stake. Imagine losing your job, your family, even your life. Because with crack, the next hit could be your last. I know some people for whom that really happened, too.

Remember, it starts out as a thought until you put that thought into action...We made it back to the Rehab Center just in time for dinner, and boy, was I ready to eat. We had to attend a CA (Cocaine Anonymous) meeting after dinner, and I had an assignment to finish. Talked with Susan and Deb after the meeting. After the CA meeting, we shared how we needed the program. We did not like what our lives had become. All 3 of us were looking for the same results: freedom, guidance, understanding, love, respect, and peace of mind, but we must keep in mind that everything has a price. Are we willing to accept it...acceptance.. can we let go and let God, or will we try to take control, knowing what happens every time we do?

I finished my one-step assignment today before bedtime. I don't think people really understand how terrible an addiction can be. I became powerless. I thought doing a little from time to time was my way of being in control. Anything to justify my usage was a pattern within itself. Bingeing 2 or 3 days at a time, not often, but frequently enough to keep my life out of control. I only have about 6 days left. I am anxious and nervous that soon, I will be back in the real world. No one is looking over my shoulders. I must be honest with myself no bull crap.

I also found out today that I will be in an aftercare program for 2 months, but that's small stuff, right? I still have some patching up to do with Brenda; I will be taking it one day at a time, 1 step at a time. Don't overload your plate. These things take TIME. Time is a word I remember from my 1st rehab program. So, you see, I did get something out of the program. How do I get the trust and the love back? I say, remember the word TIME. "Things I Must Earn" That phrase has stuck with me a long time. No pun intended. Time will heal wounds because people get hurt in the process of using drugs. We inflict wounds upon people, and it takes time for them to heal. These things don't happen on their own; they need help from you. We as addicts must keep in mind that recovery is an action program; sitting around hoping and praying will not get it done. How many times in your use of your drugs of choice has the drug just manifested itself before you, not one time? This includes alcoholics as well.

What I am trying to say is you have to use that same energy that you used to get drugs; now you have to use that energy and know how to quit them. Get clean and sober, if not clean get sober. When we are using ourselves, we are putting forth efforts; we lie... effort, we cheat... effort, we steal... effort or whatever. An effort of some kind was made, and you were rewarded for your efforts; we were putting in the effort for all the wrong reasons. Try putting forth efforts for the right reasons.

I talked with Brenda before the evening was over. I did not talk for very long because I had an assignment to finish. I had a fear about coming here, but now I have a certain fear about leaving and going home. I still say options, choices, and destiny brought me here. We have a Native Indian counselor who comes on the weekend; he is a recovering addict. It was mesmerizing to me to listen to him talk. He talked with us about Spirituality.

The Native Indians, I always saw them as being deeply rooted in spirituality...and I must say this comes from me watching movies. But the counselor who stood before us was real, and so was his presentation. His image sticks with me, as do his words. I enjoyed listening to him. Mike C also checked out today after we got back from our tour of downtown Salt Lake City, Utah. I didn't get to know him that well, but I did enjoy the tour; thanks, Mike.

There is something about being here that has been spellbinding. I have never been around a group of people with whom I have felt chemistry, like the group that I met here at the program. Maybe it's because we are all a bunch of drunks, pill poppers, and crack smokers who understand one another. Maybe it's because we feel the magic of the spirits, or maybe we believe in ourselves and our God as we know him.

Day 17... I have been waiting for it to snow ever since I arrived, here it seems. Skies are gummy-looking nearly every day. Well, last night we got that snow; now I am hoping that we don't get any more. I only have a few days to go; I don't want to get snowed in and not be able to leave Utah. I guess I have been here too long. Every day seems to be like the other, repetitive, and I am homesick. Hard to stay focused. People leaving the treatment center, people coming into the treatment center, it's a revolving door. A guy from Texas arrived today, and he is 59 years old. Lord, I do not want to be 59 years old with an addiction of any kind. I went over and introduced myself. He didn't say much, but I understood. I felt the same way when I arrived about 17 days ago. A couple of bad meals, he'll be just fine.

I talked with one of my counselors today; she is supposed to set up a conference with Brenda and me. Not looking forward to that, but I guess I am being selfish. What the counselor is doing is part of the program. I am aware that Brenda has things on her mind she would like to discuss. After all, I did leave her holding the bag, as they say. She asked for none of this type of behavior in the marriage... She was pretty pissed when I left, and I am saying that as mildly I can.

It's a very busy day. Jim T is leaving today—my coleader. Jim has been a part of my group since I arrived. I have enjoyed sharing with Jim. Jim is a laid-back older fellow, a railroad worker. Nothing seems to rattle him as long as he has a toothpick in his mouth. I think that toothpick is his security blanket. Things want to be the same when he leaves, but we can't stay here forever. I can begin to feel the human bond between us drifting apart. We must make the bond last spiritually in our hearts; those were words the Native Indian had spoken.

Over half the people I knew in my group are gone. It's just about a whole new group. We elected new leaders today, even my time is about up. I talked to Brenda today, and she said she was ready for me to come home; like I can, I can just walk out here. I hope when I do get home, she will not try to work my program like the other time I was in treatment. I will really have to talk to her about boundaries, or at least I hope my counselor does. I don't want to start an argument there.

Day 18... 3 days left, and today was quite a day. You should know now how our days began: breakfast, meditation, medications. Today I did my step 2, and several people jumped my butt. My assignment was to write a goodbye letter, like a Dear John letter, to my drug of choice.

What you will read next is what I wrote word for word...

Dear Crack,

I hate to think I will never be able to drink a beer again for the rest of my life, for the beer may trigger my addiction. This is the end of what I thought was a good relationship.

I admit you really had me fooled into thinking you were what I needed to get me through certain times. You made me feel good when I was feeling bad and bad when I was feeling good. You really know how to mess with my emotions.

So many times in my life, you did nothing but cause me problems. You would leave me feeling angry and frustrated, leaving me alone to face the mess you created. I would put you down for a while, but you always would resurface. You would even come to me in my dreams, letting me know you are always present.

I really hate you for making me feel this way. You made my life unbearable at times. I've got to let you go.

I know there is someone else out there saying what I usually say: I can handle it, or I will do it on the weekend only. I can quit any time I want.

Well, I am letting you know I quit you and got help.

Jimmy M.

Well, I guess I did not express myself too clearly because they said not one time did I mention drugs. What? I admit it made me a little hot under the collar; I thanked the group for calling me out. Connie, one of the therapists, left today; everybody loved Connie. She is a very sweet person in every aspect. We could do nothing but wish her the best. She gave us a lot of insight on how to deal with everyday issues. She felt everyone was special and that God had a plan for all of us. She loved her meditation music, which sounded weird to me. Connie taught me a lot about boundaries and feelings. Connie, I thank you.

A lot of tension seemed to have built up today with everybody. It seemed to start yesterday with Ron and Earnest. People are concerned about their personal affairs outside of the program. Some people want answers right away; some things take time. Some were too anxious, and some did not have a clue; they had mainly just arrived. I talked with Earnest and told him to be patient. There were a lot of people checking in for treatment; most of their drugs of choice were OxyContin. So many people had checked in, and they put some in hotels. Now, not all patients were "addicts." I found out later that some were mental patients... remember Steve, my first night here?

Some were concerned because they had not seen their doctor. I personally praise the staff. I think they were doing a fantastic job handling a lot of issues, dealing with a bunch of addicts and alcoholics; you can't please everyone.

I talked with Brenda today; she told me about the bad weather they were having in Arkansas. It was a winter storm, and several people had died. Now, that is really strange. I am looking forward to the snow here in Utah when it's snowing all over the state of Arkansas. Oh well, Jim T and I got on the subject of going to CA and NA meetings. We talked about how we hated to attend them because all addicts did was tell war stories. I hate war stories. They are reminders of my used days.

They call that romancing the drug, memories of the time you were together, and how it made you feel. I have not reached that point where I don't think about it; I am not there yet. We are trying to get those thoughts out of our heads by not thinking about them. It's like having a love affair with someone, and you can't see them anymore because it's life-threatening. I have accepted that I must do what is needed to recover and stay recovered.

One of the first things they want us to do is find a sponsor and a CA or NA meeting within so many days of getting out of treatment. I met with a lot of the staff today. One of the counselors mentioned I only had about four days left. She wanted to know what my plans concerning my marriage were. I jokingly said I wanted to know them, too.

I did not want our marriage to fail, and I felt Brenda felt the same way. I believed it was something we both had to work on together. We both needed counseling. I was getting help; she had not. I'm sure resentment has built up. It won't be cake and pie when I get home. I feel there are a lot of issues with the drug and the addiction that she does not fully understand. She thinks that her love for a person is some kind of cure; it's not, but it helps. It takes more than that. In the past, she tried to work my program for me. They would ask me a question, and she would answer. They would ask me if I had any meetings; she would answer. She did all the things a concerned person would do. She tried to carry the burden for me. One of the counselors asked her to please let me answer. She told me she didn't like his attitude. I love my wife dearly; we will work through this.

Issues really kept popping up today. As usual, we had our men's group when Earnest mentioned he was ready to go home. He was tired of everybody. You could hear the frustration in his voice. He realized his own wrongdoing was what got him from Texas to Utah. Well, welcome to the club, I said to Earnest. I want to be around my people as well, I said. Some of the white people offensively took this, since Earnest and I are the only black people at the Rehab center, really, nowhere else, no staff, no van drivers... The only person I saw of color was the young lady from the Philippines whom I had spoken about before. They took it as if we wanted to be around black people. All Earnest and I were saying was we wanted to be around our family, and by the way, my family is white.

To make light of everything, I went on to tell them the story about when the railroad helpline called to tell me I was going to Utah. I told the lady on the phone, You've got to be kidding. I said I don't know anybody in Utah. The only black person I know of from Utah is Carl Malone, and I don't think he will be at the rehab center; joking, of course. Earnest gave me a high five. You know how we brothers do it. I guess that offended them. I wonder if I had told them that my family was white, would that have offended them as well? It turned into a shouting match before it was over, but cooler heads prevailed. Earnest and I apologize if our actions may have offended anyone.

The rest of the day went smoothly. Ben D. and Jim T. got their coins. I wish them both the best.

Day 19... As I sat and pondered my thoughts while having a good breakfast, I realized that the longer you are here, the better the food tastes. I know it will be sad leaving. I have met some wonderful people here- a lot of good and concerned people. We have shared laughter and memories that will last a lifetime. People like the ones I have met here are hard to come by. I realize ninety-nine percent of them I may not see again; I won't say never. There are some I am closer to than others, but I have a love for them all. Sue, Ben, Jim T, Fred, Deb, all the Mikes, all 4 of them, Paul, Earnest, Jon, Ron J, Ron P, Jeff, Cory H, Steve, Rich, Mitch, Kim, Tara, Tiffany, Gary, Chad, Trent G, Kathy, Dennis, Wallace, John S and Cindi and all the newcomers. All of them have had a hand in my recovery, and I am grateful.

Got my airplane ticket info today. I will be leaving on a jet plane 3 days from now. I am looking forward to leaving; it's time to move on. I pray I can keep this positive attitude with me. I look at a lot of the younger people who are coming in, and I say I am glad to be leaving. Attitudes are different, and there is an age gap. The drug use is entirely different; there are no alcoholics; all the alcoholics were in my 21-day stay. Believe it or not, I was the only Crack user in the Rehab. It's not like it was back in the early 90s, when I was in my 1st Rehab, nothing but crack users were there. Now they are using Oxycontin, Oxycodone Hydros, Meth and the list goes on. Like I said, attitudes are different; some are court-ordered to be here, and some are here to keep from going to jail. I do understand, I am here to keep from losing my job, and I am no better than they are. But I am better than the person who has a problem and is not doing anything about it.

Today in the community, we had what we call the Bitch session. That's right Bitch session. In this section, we iron out our issues. No matter what they were, some were childish and could have been handled on an individual basis. I met the staff at Highland Ridge to discuss some of the issues. They really caught me by surprise. I hope my input was helpful. Most things were taken care of right there on the spot. That made a lot of people feel better, including me.

One of the counselors got a little unnerved today. I would say more or less stressed out; after all, he is human, dealing with human issues. We felt he was a good counselor; he would let us battle it out in group when we felt someone was being untruthful and dishonest. We all like Dennis.

Since I had a pass to leave the Facility, I went and had lunch with Steve. Steve was an outpatient; he did not live at the Facility, and he was paying out of pocket for his treatment. We went to a place called Cafe Rio. They served Mexican food. It was a popular place to eat, and there was a long line to prove it. Steve told me, "The lunch is on him; order what you want." I did. I like Steve not because he bought my lunch, but because he seemed to be a very bright young man. I never asked his age, but I would guess he was about 26 or 30 years old. He had his own business and a loving family. You would think that with the age difference, there would not be anything to talk about. But we shared a lot of laughs during our dinner. Steve shared how he wanted to get his life together, but he said, It's too much fun out here. And you could see that fun look all over his face. He was not ready for what he was trying to do, and I told him that. It was all in his conversation. He was doing the program to hold on to his family... (Please don't forget this name, Steve; it will come up again in another chapter.)

Tomorrow I get my coin; I am feeling anxious. I, along with the other guys in the apartment, stayed up late talking among ourselves about what we had to do in our lives. I think we all got the picture.

Had a late-night talk with Brenda. She has a better tone in her voice. I always knew she would be strong; that's one of her qualities. Only 2 days left, this ride is coming to an end. In spite of the reason for my being here, it has been fun and a learning experience. I have learn things about myself, my triggers, my boundaries and my behaviors. I finished my aftercare program plan. I struggled with it, but I finished. The bottom line is to do the things you promised yourself. I promised myself I would have 25 meetings in 90 days. I know it sounds like a cop-out when the program requires you to do 90, but that is not an impossible task. I don't want to make a promise I may not be able to keep. I don't want to get overburdened, so I set my boundaries. Boundaries are the teachings from our counselors. I am just being honest.

Today was really upbeat. Everyone seemed in a joyous mood. I said goodbye to some of the staff who would be off for the weekend. I thanked them for caring and making us feel special, and I said that we were worth the effort. They wished me good luck going forward. Some of them even signed my Blue Book. Kim, Cory, and Paul had their coining. "Coining" is nothing but a coin that represents the fact that you have finished the initial steps of the program. In my case, it would be a 21-day coin; I'm not sure if theirs is the same since some were court-ordered. Paul told me he was really concerned about leaving; I am sure he understood he can't stay here the rest of his life. I spent most of the day signing books by my peers and saying goodbye. Some would be leaving to go home, and some would be going to another phase of the program. Some would be going to a halfway house. We know we may never see each other again. We talk about how our lives have changed in such a short time, and that, deep down inside, we have found a new way to deal with certain life issues. We found something as a group that we should cherish for the rest of our lives.

Day 20... Only 1 day left. I am mainly going through the formalities. We, as a group, went on a tour, one I will never forget. We went to Park City, Utah. This is a beautiful place. It's like walking in a Christmas postcard. Narrow streets, gift shops, boutique shops, and coffee shops remind me of a scene from a movie. Mountains surrounded the entire city. Everywhere you looked, there was movement: people walking, people skiing, and snowboarders on snow-covered slopes. There was a certain type of serenity in just being here. The image of this place will forever be etched in my mind. It's like a dream. Brenda and Drake, my grandson, would love this place. It's beautiful. We, the group, visited where the 2002 Winter Olympics were held. We saw the ski jump and the downhill slope. You would have to see it for yourself; this place is like Christmas all year long. In fact, it was late February, and Christmas decorations were still up; what a scene. We really had a fun day, grown kids on a field trip in a van that had the words mental health written on the side. We stopped at a Walmart, and people really thought we were from a mental health institution.

We got back to Highland Ridge at bout 5:30 pm. There was nothing to do the rest of the evening. Some watched TV, some played games. As I sat, I began to wonder about the days ahead. Getting back into the flow of life. Taking on life's perils and adventures. I am thinking about getting a sponsor and getting started with my program. Don't want to rush things a day at a time. I say one thing at a time, take them as they come, and prepare for others. I really want to work on a good program. I don't want to go overboard with it; nice and steady. It came about 2 inches of snow today as we were on tour; I was getting a little concerned because I will be leaving in a day, and it's snowing. I don't want to be snowed in. I am ready to go home. The snow this time only lasted about an hour; in Utah, they call these snow showers; in Arkansas, it's called a school closing.

I left the rest of the group after dinner; I walked over to my apartment to turn in early and get a good night's sleep. Today had been a very busy day, with the tour of Park City and the outing to Walmart. I also got my 21-day coins for completing the program. I did all I could to keep from crying, but my tears were beginning to flow. I know some probably thought I was trying to make a lasting impression, but I was not. I just hoped I touched someone like members of the group had touched me. I will miss everyone I met here. I hope they got out of the program what they put in, and hopefully, it will guide them in their life through the roads ahead. To me, it was to find some inner peace, forgive myself for my past actions, and ask the ones I may have hurt for forgiveness. I really felt empty when I first arrived; today, I don't feel that way; I am feeling quite tranquil. No fear, just great expectations for my future.

Day 21.... the day I have been working towards, the last day. My airplane leaves at 10:15 am and I have my ticket to fly. I went to my last meditation and ate my last meal in the cafeteria. Sue and Deb joined me. They told me about Loyola's relapse. Loyola was in the aftercare program; she had gotten out of Highland Ridge about 2 weeks earlier. We were discussing her as she walked up. She immediately started crying. Deb and Sue gave Loyola a big, tearful hug. You could see the despair on Loyola's face. I gave her words of wisdom: *Don't give up on yourself.* I felt she was strong because she came back. Wish I could have lifted her spirits more. I said goodbye to Earnest and told him to say goodbye to weed, and I jokingly told him *Hey brother, you are on your own.* That got me a high five and a brotherly hug. I gave Sue and Deb my final goodbye hug and wished them and their family the best. Proceed to the nurse's station to give my urine sample and do my final paperwork.

Pete, the guy who picked me up in the middle of the world on my arrival this time, picked me up at the front door. He was in a talkative mood, and so was I this time. We made it to the airport with time to spare. We said our goodbyes, and he wished me luck in life. Glad I got to the airport with time to spare, there was a long line. All I was hoping for was a window seat; like a kid, I love watching the scenery when the airplane takes off. My flight was headed to Phoenix and from there to Little Rock. I admit I am not much of a flyer. I have a fear of flying, but when your time is up, your time is up, whether you are flying or walking, you have gotta go. I am more concerned about the plane crashing than I am about terrorists. Once I am in the air, I am ok. I made it to Phoenix on time. I thought the landing was really rough, and so were about another 20 or 30 people. We were all looking at each other, putting on the brakes, and bouncing around. I would say the landing got everyone's attention.

I landed in Phoenix, and I received very special attention at the Phoenix airport. I was pulled over to the side and searched thoroughly. I really thought I was going to miss my flight. They kept huddling up, looking in my direction, and pointing. Those were not good signs. They had me take everything out of my carry-on, pull off my shoes, and run the scanner over me again. I had a shopping bag with some of my dirty clothes and a little contraband from the rehab center. I had confiscated some food from our community commissary back at the Rehab. I had no money, so I bought the candy and crackers so I would not get hungry. I probably had enough snacks to last three or four days, so I took a little more than I needed for a short flight. God forgive me... life goes on.

As I sat staring out the window at God, who knows what state below we were passing over, I was thinking about the task ahead. As my daddy would say, Son, school is out; it's time to go to work. My thoughts were also on the people I left behind at the treatment center. I asked myself, What did I get out of all this? Did I give it my best? Was I honest with myself? I would certainly want to believe I did. I came into the program searching for the inner person I had lost doing crack cocaine. I had really lost touch with the goodness of God for other pleasures. I was making my own path. I had really gotten away from my upbringing. God was in my life, but I was not into God. But when you get in a tight spot, you cry out to God. Yes, that's what I did, always crying out and making promises to God. As long as I was cracking, I felt no need for God. Really, it was more shame than anything. Pure insanity, again and again. God was really watching over me. Maybe so, I believe it depends on your state of mind. Like I said earlier, a lot of people will blame God for the bad things that happen in their lives. I am responsible for my actions, not God. I have the right to ruin my life, not someone else's; this applies to everyone. I believe we control the spirits that live within us; God controls the universe. We are all elements of that Universe. We all like to feel we are worth the effort of just being, whether we are rich, poor, young, or old.

Well, I finally made it to Little Rock Airport. The crew was waiting for me. Brenda, Drake and Mattie had hugs and kisses. It was good to see them, and I was glad the kids came along with her; it helped to break the tension. I finally made it home, and there were reminders everywhere that it had been a winter storm in Arkansas. My house surroundings were a mess from broken tree limbs. Brenda went on to tell me she had been sick and that four people had died in the storm. Inside the house were a stack of bills and no money to pay them. I found out later she had to charge food because she ran out of money. All of a sudden, a feeling of guilt came over me ...but... I paused and thought to myself, it's time to see what I am made of. I got to see if my mojo is working. My first solution was to do nothing, that's right, absolutely nothing, nothing until tomorrow. I left my bags packed. Brenda had rented some movies during the snow. I picked out a movie, and we watched it. I said to myself, it is good to be home.

The next morning, I contacted my EAP (Employee Assistance Program) to let them know I had returned home and I was requesting some time off before I go back to work. I had some business matters to attend to. I needed to start by getting my house in order with bills and picking up dead limbs. The snow had broken down around the house. I hate looking at dirty snow; the snow back in Utah seemed white as snow. A couple of days have passed; I hate to hear the mail truck because it... more bills. I went to my aftercare program 4 days after getting home at a place called Bridge Way in Little Rock, Arkansas. The first meeting was quite pleasant. I expected to see Ben D, whom I met in the Utah program. He lived in Little Rock,

Arkansas, and worked for the same railroad I worked for. I mentioned that to Fran, the counselor. She said she was expecting him, but he had not shown up.

I am very concerned about Brenda. I have talked to her about seeing a therapist; she seems down in the dumps. She is feeling some kind of way. She seems quite edgy, and I am finding it hard to converse with her. I am really confused about the bill situation, I told Brenda. You told me certain bills were paid when we talked over the phone, but it seems they were not. She told me I was acting like nothing ever happened. I admit I may have been acting that way because I refuse to beat myself up about it. I am trying to move forward in a tactful way, but all of a sudden, things are falling apart, and I am overreacting. I feel the pressure. I feel the weight; I just need a little time for things to jell. I can't get Brenda motivated; hell, I can't get myself motivated. It's still a mess around the place. I need to do something to get my mind off this crap. All this is nothing but fallout from my drug use. There will be plenty more days like this. I must learn how to cope with them.

Nearly a week has gone by, and I have not gotten a sponsor. I did get a chance to talk with my EAP; I am slated to go back to work in April of this year. I've got a little over 40 days, which gives me more time to get things in order and make adjustments. I finally talked to a doctor, whom a friend I knew had mentioned. I went by and talked to him; he had 12 months of sobriety. But I could sort of tell by his language that he was not completely devoted to his program. I had no problem with that; that's his issue.

He had certain issues that he was dealing with, as well as his pros and cons about the program. He also went to Bridge Way afterward. We did have a conversation about the things I needed to do to live a healthy lifestyle. We talked whenever I would see him at the aftercare. He really helped me settle down and get a grip on my situation.

I did some calling around and checking the local newspapers for AA and CA meetings in my area. Nearly a week has passed, and I have not attended a meeting. I promised myself two meetings a week, but so far, I have fallen short. But I have tried. I do a little reading in my so-called Blue Book, but that's not the satisfaction I am looking for. I must learn to turn the uncontrollable over to my higher power. I know God is working with me on this.

Ron P. from Louisiana called. Ron was with me in the Utah program. He called to tell me everything was okay. Ron was a straight shooter; he told it like he saw it. We talked briefly; he was on his way to a halfway house in Louisiana. I told him that if he was ever in my area, he should holla at me. I was glad to hear from him, glad to know he was doing something on the positive side of life. I also got a call from Sue; she left about a week after I did. Sue told me the crew had dispersed; all new people had basically arrived. She said the place had really changed in just one week.

It seems I am getting as big as a house ever since I stopped smoking crack and cigarettes. Yes, I quit smoking cigarettes as well. One thing I learned from smoking crack is to never take your cigarettes with you to a crack house. When you come out, you have no cigarettes, just an empty package. Being in the treatment center and eating three healthy meals a day will put some weight on you. I have gained nearly 15 pounds; that's another issue to work on. I've got to do something to keep from getting bored. So I joined the Wellness Center. It's free; I might as well take advantage of it. I am very concerned about my financial situation. I really screwed up a good paycheck the week before I went into the rehab program. I blame all the bills on my stupidity, and they are still piling up. I understand it will be a good two weeks before I get a sick benefit check. Boy, do we need it? Brenda gets disability, but that does not begin to cover our household expenses. I am beginning to look around the house for things to take to the pawn shop. In all my use, I never carried anything to a pawn shop. I did lose items to crack dealers for little or nothing. I am lucky I did not lose my life or my job, and I am here now trying to save all three: life, job, and marriage. God truly watches over me; I have always had that belief.

I sit and ponder how life will be without that occasional beer or wine, especially when Brenda and I dine out. It seemed like drinking a beer and watching football with the fellows was so relaxing; I had taken away one of my joys in life. Brenda and I would always share a bottle of wine on our way to the casino in Mississippi. It was a good conversation, talking and reminiscing about things gone by. It made the trip so enjoyable. Brenda was not a drinker or a user. She often cautioned me about drinking. She felt it led me back to smoking crack. I disagree with that then, and I disagree now. It is a shame that we, as addicts, cannot enjoy sociable drinking, but it does feel good knowing that I can live a productive and enjoyable life without the drinking and drugs. Is this dream impossible? I think not.

As days pass by, my life seems to be getting back to some normality, or as normal as it can be for now. Nearly two weeks have passed. I still do not have a sponsor, nor have I attended any AA or CA meetings. We drive once a week to Little Rock for counseling. I am not sweating it just yet. I should have gone to church last Sunday, but I didn't. No reason why. I made a promise to myself that I would...

well, that didn't happen... just a broken promise. Instead, I carried my bass boat out to run it. It had been setting up all winter. I was thinking about selling my boat to catch up on my bills. Lately, it had just been sitting idle. It was a lot of family fun during the summer months. We would carry it to Hot Springs, Arkansas, on outings. The kids and my wife loved skiing and fishing. As for me, I went fishing.

I found 20 dollars in one of my clothes drawers; believe me, that was all we had to our name. I felt a big feeling of guilt and remorse because I had created the situation that we were living in. My family did not deserve this. These are the guilt trips I must conquer. I went to the Family Church, a church I had attended a time or two. Let's be honest, I struggle with the Church but not with God.

Going to church today turned out to be very rewarding. I said to myself, I must be going about this all wrong, and at that very moment, I saw an old friend. I asked him about AA and CA meetings in Pine Bluff, Arkansas. As this friend and I were talking, a friend of his passed by. Is it not strange how people are super friendly on church grounds, but see you in the grocery store, and they hardly speak? Maybe I have a problem with people. Anyway, back to the story: his friend was a counselor at DHS (Department of Human Services). We all conversed. I introduced myself and told him about my issues and my situation regarding getting a sponsor and attending AA and CA meetings. He took my number and promised to get me a list of AA and CA meetings in the city of Pine Bluff.

Is it not strange how things work out? The church had a good service. It was about passion for God and passion for one another. Drugs take away passion; they even take away God from your mindset and displace it with dishonesty, hopelessness, and a feeling of culpability. We, as humans, must learn to put our faith in God and start believing in ourselves. Ask God to strengthen you. You have strength, but it's weak. A weak battery doesn't start any car; you follow me? When you choose to do drugs or drink excessively, you are choosing not to be. You are choosing to escape. I am sure you have heard someone say, That's the alcohol speaking, He ain't himself when he/she is drinking, or They were on drugs; that's the reason they did that. Even society will let you use that as an excuse in a court of law. They will give you an option to go seek help. I am so glad my job had options set in place. Do you have options in your life?

I got a call from Jim T today. He told me he had talked to Sue and Deb. He said Deb was going to a women's shelter in California. He informed me about all the gossip that was taking place back at the Rehab center. He said it was a totally new group of patients and that things had changed. He and Sue were doing their care program at the hospital. Jim felt the same as I did; we believed there was a certain mystic in the atmosphere when our group was there. When each one of us departed, we carried a little bit of that mystic with us. I mentioned to him I had talked with Trent G. It was nice to hear from Trent. I had a pleasant conversation with his wife; I was elated to know that he was doing well. Trent's wife mentioned they had a new member of the family; they had adopted a girl into their family. Trent had mentioned to me that when we were back in Utah, they had planned on adopting. They already had a daughter. I told JimT that I was looking forward to the new challenges ahead; there are going to be some surprises, but I am sure to stay prepared. One day at a time, Jim said. March 11, 2003, why did I mention this day, you may have asked? Well, today will be our 11th wedding anniversary. I also remember my 9th anniversary, which was the one where I sent a dozen roses, and I showed up 2 days later. That's right, 2 days later.

I went on a smoking binge, unforgettable and possibly unforgivable in some marriages. It was something about special occasions I would seem to screw up. On another occasion, she had gallbladder surgery. What I do, I'll screw up. She had every reason to kick my ass to the curb. Once I took that 1st hit, the chase is on. If she merely mentioned going out of town, my knees would get weak. I always found a way to screw up. My crack usage went on for a good 11 to 12 years. I had some breaks in between; I would say the longest I ever went without using in that span was about 3 years.

As you can see, I am trying to justify, but with crack, the bad outweighs the good. Whether I smoked every day or every now and then, there was no justification for my actions. Before I went to the Rehab in Utah this last time, I tried all the little dos and don'ts to keep from using. I tried letting her control the financing. Hell, that really was not working. What man wants to work and not have control of his money? That really caused more problems than before. I was always arguing with her about certain bills not getting paid on time. I was really setting her up so I could get control of the money. When I knew all the time that the money in my pocket was a big mistake, all of this action rocked on for a while. Until it really came to a head in January of 2003

That's when I cried out for help. I had had enough. The only way to beat any addiction is to admit you have a problem, surrender, tap out, and give up.

I hated going to those aftercare meetings and listening to other people's war stories. I hated war stories. Brenda had her issues; she did not like going either. They were always putting her in check by telling her certain dos and don'ts she had to follow to help ensure my sobriety. I don't think Brenda took that too kindly. We would sometimes have a heated argument on our way home from the meetings; it became stressful. I hated going to them for just that reason.

I felt I was getting nowhere. 2 weeks have passed by, and there is still no sponsor, and there is still no AA and CA meeting. We were bogged down with bills and no money. I am having to borrow money just to get to my aftercare program. My disability insurance paperwork had not been received. I have to learn to be patient, but that's getting thin. I thought about the three p's: passion, people and patience. I must develop a passion for wanting to get my life back in order. I must learn to deal with people on a different level, remember that not all things will work in my favor simply because I stop using them, and I must have patience for the process to work. Right now, I am dealing with all three.

I called another person someone from the church had mentioned. All I got was his answering machine; I left my number, hoping he might call me. I have talked with several people now, trying to get a sponsor and meeting locations. A couple more days went by, and a guy I had talked with earlier at Family Church called and invited me to Family Church to a men's program called Iron Man. I was a little hesitant at first, but I did accept his invitation. The all-male service was gratifying. The message was all things passion. Having a passion for God, getting passion in our lives for our family, our job, and our church. Sitting there listening to the minister, I realized I had lost passion for a lot of things in my life: family values, job, self and church. That's when I asked myself what I have a passion for. How would I regain that desire within me? I do feel my self-esteem picking up, but my motivation is slacking. I have begun to plan my time for doing something constructive, not just sitting around the house watching television and playing video games.

I nearly made it to my 1st AA meeting tonight, but there was a time that caused me to miss it. I was an hour late. I hung around and mingled with the group that was there, about seven of them. I introduced myself, and they gave me a schedule for when they would meet. Their meeting place was in a public library. I really felt good about meeting and talking with them. I thought to myself that I had nearly 30 days of being drug-free; I thanked God for my strength and vowed to attend their meetings.

Another week has passed, and I am getting a break from my bills. My worker's insurance disability has kicked in. Boy, am I glad. Getting that check in the mail was a welcome, and the good thing about it is that I don't have to pay any drug dealer. Thank you, God. I take my days as they come. God knows my needs, and every day, he supplies them.

I finally made it to my first meeting, which was somewhat of a relief. There were only seven of us there. I was nervous, and I was glad to be there; they gave me a warm welcome. I went to my 2nd meeting the same week at the same location. We meet on Thursdays and Saturdays. I was finally keeping my word, showing up on time. It was good to be part of something positive.

I still have sick dreams, dreams of smoking crack, dreams that literally wake me up or that I wake myself up. I'm sure over time, these dreams will cease. I had them when I was back at the treatment center. Thank God they are just dreams. I have enough dreams to last me. Does this mean I am getting weaker or stronger? My days are not filled with cravings, but some cravings do come from time to time. I do keep myself quite busy. I have cleaned up all the limbs from the snowstorm. I go to the gym 2 to 3 times a week. I would imagine Brenda gets a little uneasy when I leave the house. I try to assure her the best I can that I am going to be alright; no worries. Building up trust is a job. It takes days, weeks, months, and sometimes years, and it can all be destroyed in a day, hell, less than that. I wanted to be trusted by my family and by the people who knew me. I even wanted to be trusted by the drug dealers. When I was using, I didn't have money all the time. A person needs a line of credit. I know that sounds terrible, but that's the truth. I wish I could get more accomplished, but the lack of money is preventing it from happening. I am not upset about it. Remember, it takes T I M E.

I joined the Family Church. I am hoping to get more involved in church activities. I feel the need for fellowship and spiritual guidance. But, being honest, I have my concerns about the church and the activities that go along with it. I have my beliefs and my doubts, and I will leave it at that. I am feeling blessed and grateful that things are and will be ok, as long as I play my role. I still wonder about the people who were in the program with me. I think about how they are doing. I have plans on reading my Blue Book more, as it will be very important now that I am going to AA. I really have a hard time reading; staying focused is the big issue, not because of a lack of interest. After all, life is about making the right decisions. God gave us that free will. Have you ever made a choice or decision, and later regretted it? I am sure we all have; that's really what life is all about: making good, sound decisions. Well, that does not speak too well of me. I have made some decisions, knowing the outcome was not going to be good, knowing all the time that what I do affects other people. I made them with my job and my family, but mainly myself.

Who do you blame, yourself or God? I truly believe, and this is a fact. Whatever situation you are in right now, it is your fault, whether good or bad. We don't like taking the blame for actions when things go wrong; we put it on the Devil. No, you made a bad decision. Bad decisions have bad outcomes. I believe God will direct us through tough situations if we have faith and trust in God. It's much easier to blame someone or something else for our shortcomings, and sometimes we must realize some things were not meant to be for us. After all, we live in a construct. Maybe that's why we try to escape through drugs and alcohol, but it's all trickery. We can't escape ourselves, and we can't snap our fingers and make things go away. Silly as it may sound, I have tried doing both; yes, I have snapped my fingers and clicked my heels, but nothing happened. But I do believe being in some type of recovery program does help if you commit yourself.

Commitment is the key to change. Renew your mind. Here is a metaphor: If you hit your hand with a hammer and you know it's gonna hurt, why do you do it? Now, take that same process and apply it to drugs and alcohol. You know what the outcome is going to be, but you do it anyway. That's the construct you have to change. I have changed my patterns about certain things. There are certain streets, and even today, I don't travel down them because I don't want to wake up those old demons. I don't wash my car at certain car washes. I have changed the music I listen to. All of these things affect your thought process. I have nothing against Bobby Brown, but I don't listen to Bobby Brown. Because his music takes me back to a time when I was using. The CD of Bobby Brown got stuck in my CD player in my car. All I could hear was this song title... Every Little Step I Take. That was my crack theme song. That song triggers me this very day. I don't tempt myself anymore. I am weak, and I know it. I still have scars.

Every day living is a constant battle when you are trying to recover. You can stay in and fight, or you can bow out; it's your choice.

I am about three weeks out of the program, doing my aftercare. I still have my recurring dreams. In these dreams, I am never using; I am always in the process of trying to find crack, or what I thought was crack turned out to be something else. You know how dreams work; we all have them. I don't tell Brenda about these dreams; she may not understand, and she may take them as a sign of me wanting to use them. I received my 1st postcard from Trent G. I was glad to hear from him. It was good to know he was doing okay; there was no doubt in my mind that he would be. So now all I have to do is answer him back within thirty days.

Today is March 19, 2003. It's been 90 days without a cigarette. I have quit several times before and always seem to go back; I've got too many habits. I remember quitting cigarettes for 8 months, thinking I had kicked the habit, but I was wrong. I have not smoked a cigarette since December 19th, 2002. That date also happens to be my last binge date. It seems "smoking cigarettes" and crack cocaine went hand in hand.

To this point in my life, it has been over 13 years since I have smoked marijuana and forty days since crack. Thank God for that, but don't go patting myself on the back; this journey is just beginning. At this moment, I do feel I have made progress.

I missed my 1st outpatient treatment yesterday due to the weather, and no, that's not an excuse. The outpatient I attend is over 50 miles away, but when it's rainy, it seems farther. I don't like driving in rainy weather.

I hate getting involved in this program and not giving it my all. I told my therapist I felt I was not getting anything of substance from the treatment. My therapist said that maybe I had not reached the point yet, and who knows, others could be feeding off of you. She felt that I was selfish and did not respect other members of the group. After all, you are not the only person with issues. She suggested that I should listen more. You are not learning anything when you are talking. I went to my 2nd NA meeting with a small group, and the topic was dreams. That topic was right up my alley. I told them that I had dreams, and they seem to be becoming quite frequent. I said, in these dreams, I am surrounded by cocaine, but I can't get my hands on any of it; you know how twisted dreams can be. They are so vivid that I wake up sometimes feeling like I have used them. That's how vivid my dreams are. Some said, *Don't worry, you are not alone.*

That's the power of the addiction. It visits us in our dreams; it never rests. But with T I M E, they said the dreams will not be as frequent. You are still early in the program; life will get better if you have faith and continue to work your program. I wonder about people who are still using. How will they get better if they have not accepted the fact that they have a problem? I can only imagine how long they will last. I have been out there; I know what some of them are going through. I know the misery, the shame, the guilt. You are headed to rock bottom if you continue to use it; it doesn't matter what your drug of choice is. Prescription drugs and alcohol really fall under that same umbrella if you abuse them. I was not really aware of prescription drugs being abused until I went to rehab in Utah.

I know the feeling of feeling hopeless, not caring, but caring and praying all at the same time. When the craving really takes over, you don't care. I know I went to places to get drugs that I would not have been caught dead in. I was more concerned about getting the high than I was about my safety, my job, or even life as far as that is concerned. I had that. I pray I don't get caught with an attitude. It seemed the more I got away, the more chances I would take. I didn't care that it was a known crack house. I was determined, no matter what the consequences were. That's the mind of the addict.

I went to my 1st A A meeting tonight. Well, I must say after attending, I was a little disappointed, or maybe it was because I didn't know what to expect. Anyway, I was all pumped up and a little nervous as well. I left home feeling good. This meeting was held at one of the bigger churches in my area. I had already surmised it would be nothing like the NA group that I had attended previously. The N A group had already told me that the AA group looked upon the NA group differently... but here I go, as I pulled up on the parking lot and parked at the church. I got out and spoke with a gentleman. I asked him about the location of the AA meeting. He told me to follow him. He asked me if this was my first time coming here?... I guess it was written all over my face...I introduced myself, and he shook my hand and told me his name was Paul. I told him I was looking for an AA meeting. I mention being an addict. He quickly told me that they don't like to let addicts speak. I said, "No problem, I wasn't planning on speaking." I was beginning to think that what they said in N A was true. They see addicts differently. We both proceeded to go inside. As soon as I was inside, I saw a couple of people from NA that I knew. I grabbed a seat, and the meeting soon began. The usual circle, the circle of shame and blame. Tonight, their topic was gratitude. I was asked to introduce myself.

Remember, when in Rome, do as the Romans do... So, I introduced myself... "I'm Jimmy, and I'm an alcoholic..." Paul had warned me about what to say earlier. Now, alcoholic is a term I don't associate myself with. Why does it matter? Whether I am an addict or an alcoholic, the principle is the same. I felt I just lied in a program that practices honesty. Why should I lie about what I perceive my addiction to be? I felt like an outcast. All I could do was listen to a bunch of drunks. I felt the meeting was personal, and I was on an uninvited quest. Now I know someone will say, Why does it matter? You are there for help, and part of getting help is attending meetings. And I tell the members of the AA meeting that it should not matter to them either. Sometimes, I wish I had been an alcoholic; maybe I could have saved some money. My addiction was costly; my addiction cost me hundreds of dollars at times. Binging gone for several days, wishing and regretting it all. Trying to forget how you jus screwed up. Alcoholics black out, wake up, and don't remember anything; that doesn't happen too fast when you smoke crack cocaine. I know there were times I wished I could have blacked out or disappeared altogether. Overall, I did not accept the meeting too well. I walked out feeling bad about myself, feeling I was not being honest with myself.

I am coming up on 60 days of sobriety. I am feeling

good about my life, but I am getting a little overweight from all the inactivity, but that is expected. Feeling bad and feeling good are only temporary feelings. I am now beginning to understand what this means. Things can change very quickly. I average two to three meetings per week; I feel comfortable with that. I have had no cravings, but to say the thought of using has not crossed my mind would be a lie. I am human and still young in the program, but I stay honest with myself.

Went to a Tuesday night NA meeting. The meeting was about being powerless and life being unmanageable. When did I realize this using? I believe mine came to the forefront in 1991. It was during a period when I had just started smoking crack cocaine. I mean, I could not wait to get paid so I could smoke and get that feeling. I was single during this time period; my only responsibilities were to myself. On days without money, I would get nervous just sitting around thinking about smoking crack. That's sick; at one point in my life, I was trying to convince myself that was all I wanted to do. I just had to figure out how. Smoke crack the rest of my life. The sickness was setting in. Now, how was I going to do this? There is no such plan. You think money is the key, but it's not. If you keep doing drugs, money will disappear—people with more money than I have have failed. More money just means you fall harder. I think back to the great running back named Mercury Morris and how drugs impacted his life. Also, Dexter Manley was a beast of a football player back in the day. I don't know of any successful drug users. There were a lot of successful people who used and lost. Crack cocaine does not discriminate. But even knowing all of this, I had to discover it on my own, in my way. People believe that things happen for a reason. Some believe God tests us;

others say the Devil tempts us. I believe God doesn't put on us more than we can bear. It is we, as individuals, who burden our lives with issues that we want God to solve. We have bitten off more than we can chew or fool with something we had no business fooling with in the first place. Now we're choking on the fallout of the aftermath. All the problems I created and my creations affected others. It did not take a genius to figure that out; I admit I worked at it. It seems I could not stand things going well. I was told addicts are selfish people, always thinking of themself. We think like..How can I?.. Can you let me?.. Will you give? Those are the issues we spread. We are good at convincing ourselves and other people that we are doing the right thing and everything will be ok. I had begun to accept my life the way it was becoming. I really had to get a renewal of my mind (Jesus' teaching). Now, I have learned to accept my life the way it is. I accept it on God's terms. Do the right thing, simple. I only change the thing I can, and that is myself. As days go by, I concern myself less with the past. I have made those mistakes, asked for forgiveness, and moved on. I can't go back and redo anything I have done, it's like yesterday, it's gone; don't let it fester your mind. Sure, things flash in my mind, but today, they are less painful, which means tomorrow should be okay if I allow it. Don't let your past dictate who you are, but who you may become. I accept that, and I move on.

It's a good feeling waking up with peace of mind. I don't owe any drug dealer any money today. Today, I choose not to lie and cheat. God loves me and wants me to have a fulfilled life. Life is stressful enough as it is; why do we burden ourselves? Sometimes, all I want to do is make it through the day, whether I am drug-free or not. If I think about it, that's a good feeling if you are drug-free. I know many times I have looked at myself in the mirror and said out loud how stupid I was. How could I do that? Or, I can't believe I did that! What the hell was I thinking? I have done that more times than I care to mention. I really got tired of feeling like a fool. I felt like the biggest sucker in the world.

Remember, just because you quit using does not mean your problem will go away. It makes certain ones a little easier to face. Then again, it depends on what your problems are. I know some of the people who were in the group thought once they quit, their problems would cease; some were facing jail time, and they were naive to the fact that they still had consequences to pay. I had to face my family, my job, and people I know who know me. But most of all, I had to face myself. God is with me every step of the way.

Today is March 30, 2003, 60 days clean and sober. It is a small milestone but a big victory for me. I said I would wait one year before I would accept my coin, but what the hell? I'd better smell my flowers while I can. I must say the last 30 days have been relatively easy. I stick to the program to the best of my ability. No mind games, no people games. I have been honest and sincere with everyone I have come in contact with.

I went to an NA meeting last night; they were talking about getting sponsors. For those of you who are not familiar with the term "sponsor," a sponsor is usually someone who has worked the program, mainly all the steps. They are your go-to person when you have those weak moments when you feel you want to use or drink, whatever your addiction is. That's my next hurdle. But I am going to have to venture out to meet more people; most people in my group are young in the program. I have gotten myself into a comfort zone. They say you don't have to like the person you choose. Now I have second thoughts about this, and this is just my opinion.

I would hate to choose someone who might turn out to be a "butt hole." I don't believe that would be good for me; let me repeat that... That would not be good for me. That could create some issues for me; after all, you are sharing some personal secrets. It's hard for me to share my thoughts even with someone I know. It would really be hard sharing them with a stranger, but enough of that, T I M E will take care of that situation. Some have mentioned they have gone a whole year. I feel that when the time is right, things will fall into place. In the mean T I M E, I continue to read my big book and the Bible, go to church on occasion, do my NA meeting, and stay away from people, places, and things. I am enjoying things the way they are, and I plan on keeping this fulfillment going, no rocking the boat for me, tired of going against the grain, sick and tired of the rough edges. Staying clean and not being sick is a better way to live. Keep in mind there are three ways to do things: the right way, the wrong way, and your way; and two wrongs don't make a right.

Well, here is the situation: it's been nearly 2 months since I got out of the Rehab center. I am nearly two payments behind on my house. The water pump on my SUV is leaking, the tags on my wife's jeep are due, and credit card bills and electric bills are due. Also, my gas bill is due, and it's a big bill from the cold winter we had earlier in the year. To top it off, my funds have run out. The mailman brought more bad news today. It seems my benefits forms were not filed properly. It sounds like a song and dance, doesn't it? But my spirits are high. I recognize what's happening now as the lows and highs; the only problem with that is I created these lows and highs. Everything has its price. This is the price you pay when you are using. I hate that innocent parties have to pay; the family did not sign up for this. I know things will get better, so keep my head up. I am just paying some of the price for my drug use. I feel good mentally; financially, I am hurting.

Today, I came really close to drinking a beer, I mean, really close. I really had no craving ...this may sound crazy, but it is true. I was doing some yard work in the front yard. The temperature was about 75 degrees, a really nice spring day. My neighbor from across the street was walking across the street with a cold beer in his hand. He popped the cap. I heard the sound of the beer being opened... If you drink beer, you know that sound... Yeah, that's it. The beer can was so cold that I could see the condensation dripping from the can. For a few seconds there, my mind went south —I mean dirty south. I thought about how I could drink one beer, and no one would know it. Know one but me... But up until now, I have been honest; I'm not about to spoil that. In the past, I would let my stinking thinking get the best of me, but I made it through that situation. Today, I said a little prayer, thanking God for allowing me to use my ability to react differently. Just like you talk yourself into something, you can also talk yourself out of it.

I've got about 15 days before I go back to work. Money around here is past low. I am still trying to sell my boat; a few lookers but no buyers. I talked with an auto mechanic at a nearby auto shop about repairing my SUV. He worked something out with me; I was grateful for that. Being off from work every day is not easy. But it gives me a lot to look forward to when I retire; I need to find things that keep me busy, trying to keep things off my mind that are depressing. Brenda has been overwhelmingly supportive. But some days, I think we are getting on each other's nerves; I must admit she is getting on my nerves. The war is going on in Iraq, which keeps her occupied watching TV. I guess I am feeling a little guilty, our youngest son is over there. He is in the Persian Gulf, more or less. I pray for his safety; he is my fishing buddy, and we have had great times on the lake. I realize he has a commitment, and it's a job. God will take care of him. I believe this. Brenda and I don't see eye to eye on the war situation. But I do support the troops. Nothing good comes out of a war. I am sure you have heard the phrase I am having a normal.Well, now ordinary days are what I have. But I can still remember some days that were not so normal for a sane person from my point of view, anyway. I remember back in 1997 when I went on a 2-day binge. To be honest, my activity was kind of slow; I had cleaned up my act quite a bit. But my mind was still infested with the thought of using. I really felt good about life during this time. My job was going well. I was a supervisor, things were really going well, and I was dealing with my demons the best I could. I remember getting off from work and showing up 2 days later. I had gone on a 2-day binge. The sadness of a binge is when it's over, and reality kicks in. You've got no more money to buy another hit, that morning sun is hitting you in the face, and you've got to go home. I have been in this situation before, and I know the scene at home won't be nice. As I pulled up at home, Brenda met me in the driveway.I tell you that woman was madder than a wet hen. She started questioning me and cussing me to the high heavens. I had no defense, and I spoke very little. I did my usual, and I started lying. We argued for about thirty minutes back and forth. I was a total wreck. She did not deserve what I was putting her through. She told me to get my things and leave. Believe it or not, those were the words I really wanted to hear. I did not have the courage to leave on my own accord. Believe it or not, I really only came home just to get the money I had hidden. I would always hide money from her, not from myself. Like any addict, I had my schemes; every addict does. I always figured that if I could outlast the argument, I would be okay. I was not as fearful of her as I used to be. A lot of times, I would just ride, too fearful to go home. Like a kid who has stayed out and played too long, and momma is gonna whip your but when you get home. Brenda would get pretty nasty, in fact, downright ugly.She called the police on me a time before, and the police made me leave. One time before, when I screwed up so badly, she fooled me like we were going for a ride to talk things over. Instead, she carried me down to the police station and told me to get my black ass out and go turn myself in, and if I didn't, she was going to blow the car horn until the police came out. It took all the lying, promises, begging, and crying to convince her not to do that. I don't make promises today. I used them all up that night. On another occasion, she took a swing at me with a poker iron; she would try to hit me with anything she had in her hand. I understood her anger. Lord knows I did. She swung at me with the poking iron from the fireplace. I am talking about a rod about half an inch in diameter; I so happen to block the rod with my forearm. She was swinging for my head. Several days later, I happened to pick up the poking iron, and I could not believe what I saw. The poking iron she was using was bent from her hitting my forearm. If that had hit my head, I would not be here today. On this same particular night, the police were called, and I was told to leave my house or go to jail for disturbing the peace. That was my only option. I was not in control, but I did have enough sense not to argue with the police. Now this was the tightest spot I had ever been in. That night, I saw no way out. I didn't want to cause a scene. Besides, the police were already here. So I left walking. Here I am, dirty, needing a bath; I had been out drugging that day, had no money, and she had already taken my truck keys. Now, keep in mind I have two vehicles, yet I have to leave walking from a house where I pay all the bills. This is what crack cocaine will do to you: it will put you on the streets. As I said, I left the house walking; it was about 40 degrees that morning. No money, no drugs, no idea where I am going or where to go. It seems when you come off a crack cocaine high, you are so disillusioned. All sorts of thoughts are going through your head. Things are hard to rationalize, but you try. In the background, I keep hearing this train horn blowing. My thoughts quickly came alive. All of a sudden, this crazy thought came into my head. Hey, I will catch a train, go somewhere else, and start over. That's disillusioned thinking. I will show them. To be honest, I have tried this stunt before. I once ended up in Oklahoma for a whole week... At that time, I was really stressed out; there were other issues, but none that should have landed me in Oklahoma. I really put my family and job in a bad situation. Running away sounds really good when your head is bad and you have nowhere to go, but the minute reality starts to come back, you really realize what a fool you are. How did I allow myself to get caught up in this predicament? What in the hell was I thinking? When it all boils down, I was not thinking; I was just reacting. The night I left home walking, I ended up staying in a locomotive. I followed the locomotive tracks from where I lived to where I worked. It was about a 10-mile walk. Cold and lonely and, at the moment, homeless. I stayed in a locomotive for nearly 3 days with no food, no water, and no communication. All I did was pray, cry, and sleep. These were stored locomotives; they were about three blocks from where I worked. I nearly got caught by 1 of the bosses.

They were getting parts from stored units. I was never so scared in my life. I locked the doors so they could not get in, and they never approached the cab. God really brought me through this ordeal like all the rest. I failed myself. No more war stories, I am still healing. I still have scars. It has been said that scars prove that your past really existed. I like to believe that I lost a lot of battles with drugs, but I will win my personal war against them if I stay true. *"The way a man thinks, the way he becomes. Hang with the positive. Become positive. I am slowly but surely changing my habits. Sometimes change is hard to accept, but when we do, our lives become better."*

Today is April 4, 2003. I received some sad news today about Trent G. Trent was my roommate at Highland Ridge Hospital. I talked to his wife today, and she was telling me that Trent had started drinking, had lost his job, and wanted to commit suicide. This news really saddened me to my heart. I considered Trent to be a very close person to me, even though we were miles apart. I knew how he felt about his situation in life and how his drinking was destroying his life, from family to job. He was proud of his family, and he, like me, was dealing with a lot of guilt. When we were in the treatment center, he told me a lot of his inner secrets about how he hated how things had gone in his life. I wondered sometimes if he was really honest with himself. You can fool people, but you can't fool yourself. We ended our conversation, and I wished him the best and told him to call me whenever he needed to talk and to give Trent my love. I certainly felt for Trent and his family. I pray he gets off his butt and fights back. I will always be here for you, Trent. I went to church service this past weekend. The pastor, I thought, made a very interesting point in the service. He said we all need a compass in our lives. I agree we need direction in our lives, whether we are addicts, alcoholics, or so-called "normal" people. If you are lost and have no direction, you will forever go around in circles; let that sink in for a minute. Imagine being dropped off in the woods, blindfolded, and you are told you can find your way out by going north so many miles, then going south so many miles, and you would come up on your destination. But without a compass to identify which direction is north, you will probably go around in circles, don't you agree? What I am trying to say is that God is the best compass in our lives. If we follow God's guidance, it will lead us out of the woods. For addicts and alcoholics, the A.A., C.A., and NA are designed like a compass. They help us find our way through the insanity of addiction. They also teach us to "let go and let God," and if we do not, we will forever be going around in circles. I am now a member of the Family Church, a church body that I enjoy attending. My stepson and I attended here a time or two before. If I were asked, "Why Family Church?" I would have to say atmosphere and feeling comfortable. I enjoy the way the minister guides you through the scriptures. I don't feel singled out. Sometimes church can really put you on a guilt trip. He does more teaching than preaching. His messages are quite clear to me; there are no gray areas, either you believe or you don't. It's that simple. I remember several Sundays ago, he talked about values. What do we value in our lives? There are so many things we take for granted, and when you are using drugs, you really take things for granted. The only thing that matters is using. The Pastor gave his congregation an assignment; he told us to go home and list 10 things we valued in life and the order in which they occur. This really struck me. What did I value? What is important to me? Before you read any further, take the time right now and write down the 10 things you value in life, and oh yeah... put them in order. As soon as I got home, I grabbed a pen and paper and wrote mine down.

1. God. I need God in my life for guidance, strength, and understanding. Without God, I am walking around without a compass.

2. Sobriety. This right now is one of my greatest values. Without sobriety, everything else fails.

3. Job. I need the job for the financial aspect of my life. I believe that without a job, your ambitions diminish greatly.

4. Family/Church. I need family for love and support. Family is the meaning of my worth. The church is for fellowship and worship.

5. Myself. I value myself because I am a very important being. People depend on me: my family and my job. I play a certain role in life and society.

6. Freedom. There is nothing like it. Freedom can be described in so many ways. Freedom is truly priceless.

7. Finance. Without finance, life does get complicated. I believe the finale is what you make of it. Some people can do a lot with a little, and some do a little with a lot. I admit I am a poor planner.

8. Personal Goals. We should all set personal goals, whether we reach them or not. It's having them and working toward them that matters. To reach them builds

motivation; motivation builds hope. A lot of our lives are built on hope.

9. Material Things. I like to call them worthless things because when I was using them, they really had no value. At one point in my life, material things were high on my list. Material things, I believe, in some cases, show your worth. Material things can be disruptive and cause you to lose sight of the real values in life.

10. Peace of mind. This value comes to mind if all of the above fall into place. If my life is in harmony, I should have no problem achieving peace of mind.

Those are my top ten values. Agree or disagree is not really the issue. I believe the real issue is taking the time to stop and look at your life. I dare you, at this very moment, to stop and value your life. They are inspiring to me. I believe any one of the 10 I mention will get me through a bad day if I am honest with myself.

I went to another aftercare meeting this past Tuesday, April 6th, 2003. I am still finding it hard to fit into this group. I am averaging about two meetings per week, and still no sponsor, but between A.A., NA and C.A., I am staying busy. I get a lot of insight, strength, and fellowship from the meeting. I find myself questioning if my life is getting better, or if it is certainly not getting worse. I am learning to deal with myself a whole lot better. I don't get upset over small issues. I think before I react. Sometimes, I felt like I had to be some kind of god, trying to deal with certain issues and family, and stay in control. All I was doing was losing my grip on myself. Today, I take it as it comes. The marriage has been a struggle, and I lay a lot of the blame on my feet.

To say my wife and I never have a bad day would be a denial for me. My marriage is a very important part of my life. Our marriage could use some counseling; I know my wife still feels unsure about my drug situation, and she has every right to be. She really got dumped on because of my addiction. This was my 5th aftercare meeting. I got five more to go. The program calls for me to attend 10 after-hours meetings before I can return to work. Boy, am I ready to go back to work? Today's meeting was scheduled for 5:30 pm.

I had some time to kill, so I went to a place called Arena Billiards, a local Billiard Parlor in North Little Rock. This is where I participate in pool tournaments during the summer months. This guy and I had been shooting pool for about an hour, and there was very little conversation between us. My cellphone rang. It was my niece calling, who at the time was dealing with personal issues, not drug-related. Anyway, we talked briefly on the phone; I told her I had to go to a meeting at 5:30 that evening, and we quickly ended our conversation. The person I was playing pool with overheard me say 5:30 meeting, and I guess that made him curious about who I was. I am sure, by the way I was shooting pool, he knew I was not the greatest pool player in the house. He had been kicking my butt the whole time we had been playing. I told him this would be my last game because I had a meeting to attend at 5:30 .He agreed, and as we were playing, he said I heard you mention a meeting, I guess he thought it was a business meeting. I told him reluctantly that I had to go to an aftercare meeting about recovery and that I was an addict in recovery. He said, "Don't feel like the Lone Ranger; I'm in recovery too. I have been for two years," he added. "I, along with some other guys, come here to shoot pool every other day to relieve stress." We shook hands and introduced ourselves all over again. He said, "Hello, my name is Archie."

"I'm Jimmy," I said, "Glad to meet you." He said when I mentioned 5:30, "It triggered something inside of me." He went on to tell me that he had gone to a noon meeting that day. He also told me how the AA program had changed his life. We also shared a few war stories; suddenly, I no longer felt like a stranger. We talked so much that I ended up being late for my meeting. Archie really topped my day off. We exchanged numbers and promised to stay in touch, and we did for a little while; over the years, we lost touch, but he is someone I will always remember... Archie.

"God has a strange way of putting people in our lives; this I accept."

I went on to my aftercare meeting that evening, which turned out to be quite controversial for me. I asked the question, What am I supposed to be getting out of these meetings? I see they are stressing me out and just trying to get here. No, the sooner I asked that question, I got a lot of feedback thrown my way, but not the answer I wanted to hear. Well, here I go, being selfish again. I explained to them that my finances are on hold at the moment; I had to borrow money just to get here this evening. I said it seems like I am just wasting my time. I told them I stopped at the billiard parlor to play pool and waste some time. That might have been the wrong thing to say. They hit me with questions like, "Why did you stop at the billiard parlor? Did you want to drink? Have you used? Do you have a sponsor? Why play pool in a place that serves alcohol? Remember people, places and things? Have you been going to your meetings?" I said, "Yes, 2 per week." They said, "Go to more meetings." They mention I was setting myself up for failure. They, as a group, really laid it on me. Maybe that's why I don't like these aftercare meetings. They were mostly composed of alcoholics. I was not an alcoholic, but in reality, I suffered the same issues.

My life had become unmanageable. By now, I could begin to feel drops of sweat under my armpit; you know that feeling when someone is beginning to get on your nerves. You don't have to be an addict or alcoholic for this to happen. My stinking thinking was beginning to kick in... I blurted out. I am feeling so much frustration; I feel I am no longer in control of my life. Everything is hard to deal with. At this time, the counselor who was in charge of the meeting calmed me down.

She stated that I was not allowing the program to work on its terms. She said it seems like I wanted it to work on my term, and it doesn't work that way. That's why it's called a program. It has steps you must follow. The program does not have to follow your steps. You must follow its steps. Give it time, she said, you should get a sponsor. You seem to be struggling with your addiction. Well, I spoke out again to the disgust of the group. I mentioned that I would like to get a sponsor with whom I feel comfortable...

Someone in the group shouted out principles before personalities. It should not matter. Well, I had certainly heard that before, and just like before, I tried to defend my opinion. I said to myself, personality does matter... For example, and this is true: I went to a CA meeting, this guy was there speaking, tattoos everywhere on his body, long hair, weird looking person, he talked a good program, and it appeared he had attended a lot of meetings. He also had been in and out of rehab several times. He also had been in confinement. He talked about things he liked to do when he got high; he talked about having sex with men. I am not making this stuff up. Now, this might be the type of person someone needing help might be looking for. They say, Don't judge a book by its cover, but on this one, I pass. I can't imagine myself telling my wife that I invited my sponsor to our house so she could meet me. I would tell her to try not to stare at him when he talks because he seems easily offended; oh, did I mention he went to prison for killing someone? I know it seems I am stereotyping because things are not always what they seem. Who would you ride with, a stranger or someone you know? They continued to say that who you get as your sponsor should not matter as long as they are the same sex. And that's debatable...

I had mentioned earlier how I was short on cash; after the meeting, a gentleman who was at the meeting walked up to me and gave me a twenty-dollar bill. I was stunned, and I really didn't know what to say. I didn't want to take the money, but I was really in no position to refuse. I was really flat broke. I had about 23 dollars on my credit card. I spent 10 dollars earlier playing pool. I thanked the gentleman who handed me the 20, and I promised to pay him back. I have not seen him since that day.

They say it gets better as TIME goes on, and it does. On my way home after my aftercare meeting, which is about 40 miles away, I started reflecting on things in my life. I said to myself, I am really sweating the small stuff; there are people out there who would trade their problems for mine. There are people out there who have crashed and burned. My issues are pale compared to theirs, and they aren't doing drugs; you follow what I am saying. I think about the beauty and the grace of God. The things that God does every day are that he makes sure the sun rises and shines every day, makes sure all the rivers flow, answers all prayers, makes the wind blow, and watches over the needy as well as the greedy—searching all hearts to find the pure in heart. Today, I am thankful because I find clarity in my life. I have a totally different mindset from 4 months ago. Four months ago, I had a different outlook on life. I was blind. My thoughts were dark, complete denial about my addiction; I was putting up a fight for my addiction. The best decision that I made in my life was seeking help for the darkness. Oh yeah... I thanked God for that 20 dollars and his grace and mercy.

Today is Easter, the day of the bunny rabbit. That's what my granddaughter calls it. I am a grown man, and I have not figured out yet, through all these years, what rabbits and eggs have to do with Easter. Somewhere, we missed something, or we got preached the wrong message... Anyway, it is good to be alive this Easter Sunday. Easter Sunday always brings back those childhood memories in me. Today is the day that people who normally don't go to church go to church on this particular day. I remember how my mom would say I say so, and so I thought he was dead. Plus, you wanted to look your best on Easter. I had an Easter speech, and I had to say, Practice all week to say five words and forget them on Easter Sunday when its time to say your speech; if you are raised in the south in a Baptist church you know what I am talking about... that brings laughter to my heart, and buy the way, I had an Easter basket, yeah I did... I hated that Easter basket, and we know no Easter is complete without the Easter egg hunt.

Kids are everywhere, and more eggs than they will ever eat. The church that I have been attending from time to time had a big Easter egg hunt. I don't know many people at this church; I have only been attending it for a few months, and today, it's packed. I guess things have not changed. I know a lot of faces but very few names. It seems things are still the same today as they were 40 years ago. I am just beginning to breathe... I can't remember the last time I was at church on Easter Sunday, and I'm glad to be here. The point I am trying to make is my face is a new face in the crowd, and yeah, I got on my Sunday best. I do not have a good track record when it comes to attending church, even though, as a child, my parents made me go every Sunday.

My knowledge of church and God was very limited as a child; going to church was a play period for me. Now, don't misunderstand me. I have a belief in the Creator.

I truly believe in God, but I don't believe in all the bull crap that goes on in the churches today, and that's a subject I will not dwell on.

Today is April 19th, 2003. I can truly say I have 90 days clean and sober, and it's been 110 days without a cigarette. I went to the car wash near my house to wash my vehicle. That's about all I do in the run of a day. I don't venture out visiting old friends, and I mean good old friends. I don't want any suspicion thrown at me. Brenda gets a little paranoid when I am gone for an extended period of time; this I understand. This is part of the fallout from my drug use. I got to build that trust we had back, and this takes TIME.

As I pulled into a car wash stall. I ran into an old buddy of mine that I had not seen in nearly 12 years. This was not one of my get-high buddies. He was a buddy I used to party with when I was DJing at nightclubs back in the 80s. He began to talk about the old times, a period of my life that I was not interested in conversing about, but I talked and pretended anyway. He told me that someone had told him that I was on that stuff. I said to him in an unknowing manner...in other words, I pretended I didn't know what he was talking about. But it was obvious that my business was in the streets. I said to him, "What are you talking about?" He said, " You know that crack man, you know what I am talking about." I began to tell him about my drug use and the problems it had caused me. I was by no means ready for the conversation we were getting into; it was a triggering conversation. One that I wanted to stay clear of. I really wanted to get in my vehicle and leave, but I stayed. Well, come to find out, my friend was having problems with drugs, and guess what?... That drug was crack... Yes, crack. Our lives were sort of parallel.

I knew the war stories were coming next; I hate war stories. My counselors warned me about war stories because they can have triggering effects. He went on to tell me he was retired, how much money he was drawing per month, and how much he was spending per month on smoking crack. I stayed as silent as I possibly could; I didn't debate anything. Now, I am beginning to hate that I ran into this person. I could tell from his conversation that he was still using. This guy was romancing the drug, as they say. He was making me jealous just hearing him talk about it. He had triggered me, and I let him do it by continuing to talk with him.

I finally walked away, went over, and finished washing my vehicle, hating that I had run into this person. He had really triggered me; I summarized that he was trying to get me to do the wrong thing. Like, let's get together and see what we can come up with, buddy, not today. That's how the addiction works; I was making a futile attempt at washing my vehicle. I quickly left the car wash. For the next couple of hours, I was dealing with my yesteryears. I did manage to make it through the day. It was one of the worst days I had had since I had left the treatment center back in Utah.

Today is just another day in the life of a recovering addict; today is a special day, my granddaughter's birthday. It was celebrated at one of the local parks where I live. It was also the only time Brenda and I had really spent together socializing. We had not even gone out to dinner at this point, mainly due to funds. I admit it is hard to have a conversation with her; I feel she is holding a lot of anger, and I am holding guilt and shame. I went and got help, but nobody was helping her. There is help for her, but she refuses to go.

I don't push the issue. I know it is hard for her to put trust in me this early in my recovery stage. We have sat and tried to talk, but the conversation always got a little heated. Her attitude had changed, and she had a defeated look on her face sometimes. Nothing that I was saying was giving her the feeling of trust in me. That's because, at one time, my drug use had really gotten out of hand. It had gotten to the point that I didn't apologize anymore. I figured it would be one less lie I would have to explain. Deep down inside, she never gave up on me. I always felt that way in my heart. I had asked her for forgiveness, but she would never give me an answer. It was hard to read her moods. She had threatened to leave many times. I asked her why she never did leave, and why she threatened, I asked. She said she would tell me that, hoping I would quit using, but nothing seemed to work. She said she decided to leave me alone and let me kill myself, and she said there were times she wished I had. Harsh words, but I understood and did not blame her for her actions. You can't imagine the feeling I got when I looked a family member in the eyes and told them *I am sorry* and do the same thing over and over again. All I was creating was a web of lies. I knew what I was asking for would take TIME.

I believe she had become numb to all the lies and drug use. She would often tell me, with tears in her eyes, that she could not take the lying. She told me it was like living with Dr. Jekyll and Mr. Hyde, trying to live a normal life, acting like nothing had happened and nothing was wrong. She really got upset when I would call some of the people that was in the treatment center with me in Utah. I did not try to isolate the conversation when they called, but I tried not to show a lot of joy and excitement when I talked to them. I always have some type of negative feeling once I get off the phone. I know all these things are part of recovery.

Keep coming back because it works if you work the steps, and it sucks if you don't. That phrase has given me something to believe in... myself. I believe in the program more and more. I am really looking forward to going to the NA meetings, and tonight was a good meeting. It was good to be able to vent after a stressful day. I don't have to direct my anger toward anyone; I just vent. So many times, I wished I had someone to talk with who understood what I might have been feeling or really going through, instead of just listening to what I was saying. That's where the sponsor comes in, which I have yet to get. The program gives addicts hope, something maybe we did not have before. I had never put a lot of emphasis on quitting; my energy was used on how to keep using and getting away with it. I really did not know how to quit; I had stopped several times, but I never quit. There is quite a bit of difference. This is what I was reflecting on when I left the NA meeting tonight. Things in my life were slowly beginning to take a turn; I felt I was making progress.

Today had been a good day. It was about 10 pm Saturday night, the weekend, so I might as well take advantage of the free weekend minutes on my cell phone before it gets cut off. The bill is past due. Who do I want to talk with most? I'll give Trent, my roommate back in Utah, a call since the 12th of the month has passed. I forgot to send him a postcard. I owe him a conversation. I called Trent; his wife answered the phone. I said, "Hello, this is Jimmy. May I speak with Trent?" All of a sudden, there was a moment of hesitation. She said, "Did you not hear about Trent?" For a few seconds, I went silent, and my mind quickly filled with suspicious thoughts. I knew he was having problems, and I thought maybe he had checked himself back into rehab. I was totally unprepared for what I was about to hear... His wife said Trent is no longer with us. She said Trent had taken an overdose of pills. I said, "You've got to be kidding." She told me she had been trying to get in touch with me. For the next 15 to 20 seconds, I did not hear a word she spoke. My mind quickly reflected back to the times at Highland Ridge. I remember Trent wrapping this towel around his head like a turban, the kind the men in the Middle East wear. He would take his hospital gown and put it on backward. He looked like a Guru, and when he sat, he looked like a Swami. He was the leader of our morning meditation music. He would play anything for us to meditate by Willie Nelson, Run D M C, anything as long as it was noise. He was the most lovable and the wittiest person in the group. His words were wise and encouraging, whether from a book or from his heart. I believed in Trent recovering more than myself. I felt he was really going to get it together once he got back home. He seemed to have a beautiful family; his wife was very supportive. She drove over three hundred miles from

Kanab, Utah, to Salt Lake City, Utah, to support him on family day. Whatever the reason, Trent decided to end his life, I will never know. All I can do is speculate. There were times when I had silly thoughts; I was looking for a way out. I don't know what it takes to commit an act like that. Whatever it is, I don't have it. Only Trent and God know why he did. I believe all things happen for a reason. I am sure Trent's death touched everyone who knew him, not only the people from the treatment center but also the people in the community where Trent lived. You did not have to be an addict to love him. All you needed was a heartbeat. I chose to remember Trent as a good friend. He was very inspiring to me; I thank God for gracing me with his presence and filling my life with hope and encouragement. A little fun and a lot of reality checks. I am really saddened and angry at him for doing what he did. I guess that's part of the Serenity Prayer. The part where it says help me to understand the things I cannot change... Trent, I will never forget you; you are at peace... Rest.

Nearly coming up on 90 days of my sobriety. My life still sorta sucks, but I am ok with that. My life today is much better than it was months ago. Things are going the way God has planned. To me, recovery is a process of reprogramming the mind. I believe Jesus spoke of renewing the mind. Changing a condition in which you have lived, getting away from the wall you are beating your head against. Start dealing with a different perspective. I never tried visualizing myself, nor using it. I always visualized myself using big differences. Therefore, the pattern was set in my brain. I had played it out in my brain. The pieces always seem to fit until I take that first hit. Anyone who smokes crack will tell you that first: it will kill you. If it doesn't kill you physically, it will make you mentally and spiritually sick. When it got to a point in my life where I tried to quit on my own, it was like a person trying to lose weight. The more you try to lose, the more you gain. The more I tried to quit, the more I seemed to smoke, and the more my life came out of control, the worse I felt. That's when my madness set in. That vicious cycle takes over. Coming up missing, taking off from work. I remember calling in to work to take off. I want to show you how sick I was. I called in at 2 am to take off from work. I was supposed to be there at 11 pm. I worked the graveyard shift. My dependability was fading concerning my job. But through the grace of God Almighty, I made it through some terrible personal ordeals. Being in the program for the length of time that I have been in it has given me a new vision. A vision that I must continue to work on. There is life after drugs; you just have to want to get back what you gave away.

The Wednesday and Saturday group has rented a van to go to Little Rock, Arkansas, to attend an AA meeting to get us out of the comfort zone of CA I am looking forward to it. I still have not gotten a sponsor; maybe I might meet someone at the meeting, who knows? I know I am still contemplating the sponsor situation. I have all the intentions of getting one. I'd better do it before someone in my group relapses, talking to me about it; they are really concerned about me a little too much, I think.

Today is April 25, 2003. Four more days before I return to work. The anticipation is building. I am very apprehensive about returning to work, even though my life is more stable than it was 3 months ago. Some situations are better, and some are not. Each day is a journey. Ninety days clean and sober, give or take a few more, is like reaching a small milestone, but this is a tiny step compared to what's ahead. As far as going back to work, it's something I gotta face; it comes with the territory. I wasn't this concerned when I was using; the crack kept my mind cloudy, but believe this, I never wanted to get caught, and I never wanted to lose my job or hurt anyone. My job was a very important piece of the puzzle of my life. My wife felt that if I lost my job, it would be more than I could handle. My job gave me a feeling of value. I will go back and face my coworkers with apologies; I supervised a nice group of men and women. They were my away-from-home family. I am sure they will have different thoughts and opinions, and they have that right. Besides, some will accept, some will not, and to some, it really won't matter. People in my group seem to think my job was my enabler. I won't agree or disagree with that; everyone has their opinion. But let's be truthful: it provided me the means to buy crack ...and food and shelter and all other necessities. I just made bad choices about what to spend my money on. I think the key issue with my coworkers is how I respond to them. Would you not agree?

I talked with Tiffany today; Tiffany was with me back in Utah. She told me she was 87 days clean, and life with her was okay. I said, "Good for you." She went on to tell me she was going out on a date that night. She said it was her first date in 4 months. She said it would be her first date, clean and sober. Well, if she is deciding to take that first date step, I wish her luck and best wishes.

We had a brief conversation about the members of the group. I told her about Trent; she said she had heard about it and how sad she was to hear it. It was the weekend I talked with several other people from the group in Utah; everyone said they were doing well. It was a good feeling to stay in touch with one another.

On my way to church on Sunday. It dawned on me how I felt about going to church this morning. I sort of briefly reflected back on my life before crack cocaine. I compared it to several months ago. There was a big contrast several months ago before Rehab. I would go to church, hoping that it would make me feel good about myself. But that was not working; it only made me feel worse. I felt like glass, transparent, and everybody could see right through me. I was going through a motion that had no meaning whatsoever. My mind was cloudy. I would go to church to fool those around me. It was creating an image of what I was hiding, but today is different. I have made an improvement with the help of God. My life is of value to me and my family. Life does have meaning; I may not understand it, but it does. I don't spend a lot of time dwelling on it. My days are busy. I try to fill them with days of some type of positivity. I am helping coach my grandson's Little League baseball team. Ages 6 to 9 years, and I pick him up from school, do a little tutoring, and get on the PlayStation with him. That's a lot of fun.

I also share in my NA and AA meetings, and I keep a good attitude about myself. The keyword is attitude. I don't feel the need to prove a point anymore. You can prove more by improving yourself. People notice change. They may not question you about it, but they will question someone else. In church now, my mind does not drift and wander off. I stay focused on the ministry. Get as much out of the message that I can. Yes, life does get better. As I pulled up to the church parking lot and parked, I sat for a moment. It was a windy, blustery morning. I felt calm as I watched the tree branches and leaves give way to the wind. A slight coolness was in the air; all in all, it was very peaceful. At that moment and time, my life became serene, untroubled. I believe and always will believe God has something in store for me. I am a wonderful person; I am important to me. Life is important to me.

Well, I have finally made it 90 days. It seems like a great weight has been lifted. Last night at the NA meeting, I was gifted my 90-day key tag. I made a short acceptance speech on how grateful I was to be involved in the NA program. Getting my 90-day key tag means a lot. It showed me how my life could be without the use of crack cocaine if I accepted the change. That's what recovery is about: change. Changing your way of thinking, changing your way of doing things, changing the places you might go, and changing the people that you might know.

My hobby is drawing; I will go as far as to say that I am an artist; I have a little skill. I mention that to make this point: I would spend a lot of time drawing when I moved back in with my dad out in the country. It would take me sometimes three or four days just to draw a line. I would stare at my drawing pad for a day or so before I took action. Key phrase: "Take action." You must take action for anything to be accomplished. No line would be drawn on my drawing pad unless I took action. The same principle applies to recovery; you must take action in order to get your sanity back in your life. There are guidelines for the healing process. I believe some in the program took this for granted. I confess that in my first rehab, I took a lot for granted. I put forth a piss-poor effort there, and I got pisspoor results. You get out what you put in. Once I allowed myself to absorb some knowledge, things began to change. Getting these 90 days has been a motivating factor. It's good to have 90 days.

I went to my therapist this past week. I carried Brenda; she sat in with me. She has a lot of anger stored inside. She still dwells on the past things that I did that affected her, as well as our marriage. She finds it very hard to let go. She holds on with a vengeance. I will somehow build that trust back up, and I won't lose it anymore.

Our session with the therapist turned into a tennis match, back and forth at each other. Our day up until now has been a pretty good day. It was about the second time she and I were out together since I came from Utah. I was really getting nervous sitting there trying to deal with the situation; I could feel those drops of sweat under my armpits. I was thinking this "therapist thing" was going to ruin it all. The therapist got a little testy between Brenda and me; the venting probably did her good.

After the meeting ended, Brenda and I went and had dinner at Red Lobster, one of our favorite places to eat in Little Rock, Arkansas. It was kind of strange not drinking a beer while my dinner was being prepared; I had been so used to this routine in the past. We had a good conversation over dinner, but the drive home turned into a disaster. We both ended up being angry at each other for no reason at all. Brenda loved to bring up past drama.

Regarding things that have happened, neither one of us can change the past, and neither one of us wanted to lose the argument. I admit that a lot of times, she was right and I was wrong, and while I would admit that I was wrong, I never had a rebuttal when I was right. Some of that blame goes to addiction, but mostly to my stupidity.

Nearly 100 days have gone by since this journey to recovery began, and now I am close to getting back to work. I thought getting back to work would be an easy task, but it's not. It has its procedures. I can't just go back to work because my therapist says it's okay. I have to go through the screening process. It's simply amazing that I have worked for this company for nearly 30 years and have never been screened. I guess this is a blessing for me because if I had, I would have probably been dismissed some time ago. I have been getting by on just pure luck; there is no other way to describe it. Sure, there were people on the job who had drinking issues; everybody knew who they were. But we were a very close-knit group of workers who more or less looked out for each other. I will go as far as to say some knew I had issues, but I showed up to work and did my duties. Besides, my job was considered low-key even though I was a supervisor. As long as I did not have an accident on the job, I was okay. The company department that I worked in never did surprise drug screenings. During peaceful moments in our marriage, Brenda would ask me about my use. Questions like, Were you not afraid of getting caught? Did you ever think about the embarrassment you could have caused your family and yourself? I told her, Sure, I cared.

But I was never afraid until it was all over. As long as I was high, I was just fine. I am not saying that I was fearless because I was not. I feared getting caught by the police; I feared that more than anything. I feared facing Brenda more than I can explain. If the police got me, I could not explain my way out. As far as the job was concerned, they had a drug policy in place for employees. All I had to do was commit myself and suffer through the embarrassment, which is what I am going through now. There is always something about getting away with something that makes you risk it again. It goes back to my childhood and that buttermilk. Once I got caught and my mother whipped my butt about it, I never did it again, but I had done it many times before. Brenda would ask me how I felt about fooling people who trusted me and believed in me. I told her that once I was back to reality, I really felt terrible and ashamed. You can't see the harm or the consequences when you are using; you are blinded to the realities of the consequences. All you want to do is feed the craving. You become selfish, only thinking of yourself. To someone who has never used or been addicted to anything, this makes no sense to them at all.

I have learned many things in recovery, things I took for granted, like going on a binge and not letting her know my whereabouts. That put worry on her about my well-being and my job, leaving her to cover for me at work. For all those things, I deeply apologize and regret that they happened. Those were the things that tore down the trust in our marriage. I should have gotten help long ago.

May 7th, 2003. I have finally got my chance to go back to work. I took the drug test last week, and I have been cleared to return. It's kind of funny once I think about it. When I went to take my drug screening, the guy who gave me the urine test was telling me how they test employees, when to expect a call, and when not to drink. He told me we are not supposed to call on your off days, and while you are on vacation. He said, If you are going to relax and have a beer, I should do it at least 12 hours before I return to work. I was thinking, "Why is this man telling me all this information? I don't want to know how to beat the system; that's part of what got me in here." He told me that I would be drug-tested an average of six times a year for three years. But just listening to this guy for a short period of time planted a seed in my mind. I quickly told him that I planned on staying clean, with or without the screening. I said, "It's do or die." He wished me luck.

I still continue to go to my NA meeting; I no longer have to see my Therapist or attend those group meetings. I thank God, and I mean that in a good way. People at the meeting were telling me about how happy I looked. I thanked them and told them I was happy; I was breathing freedom. The light at the end of the tunnel was getting much brighter. I feel my tomorrow will be a whole lot easier because of the positive things I do today. When you go to these meetings, you hear people talk about being clean and sober for 20 to 30 years. Well, I am 50 years old; I may not get that kind of longevity. Only God knows, but I will be working on it. Today, I am equal to the person who is 20 to 30 years old because this is a one-day-at-a-time program. If I do my part, it will work. I believe this.

In one of my recent meetings, a lady who attended said that where she lived, there was opportunity for her to use drugs all the time. She spoke about how she would come in from work, sit down to relax and watch TV, knowing what was going on on the outside. She told about how she would sit on her hands to keep from going outside to use. I totally understood where she was coming from. I lived in an apartment briefly in the early 90s. There was drug activity going on all the time. I know that a lot of times, I have taken advantage of situations because they were convenient. There were times I would not use it because it meant driving across town. During this period, I was a casual user. I was single; I had moved from the country back to the city after my father passed. I was trying to maintain a single lifestyle but was failing at it and spending money on the wrong things, living above my means. I told her she may have to weigh her options, and one option is moving if you are serious about staying clean and sober. I told her there would come a day when you wouldn't sit on your hands but use them to open your door and go outside and make a purchase, and give up the sobriety you have achieved up to a certain point. I moved, I quit smoking briefly, I told her.

Moving was a start. By moving, I was hoping to break my pattern. My patterns changed, but my habits remained the same. Back then, I was not in any kind of program; I really didn't have a clue about cleaning up my act. I would give up drugs and continue to drink, but drinking was not my thing, except for a beer or 2 playing softball or at cookouts with my friends. By drinking, I was trying to prove to myself I did not have a problem. And to this day, I still say drinking was not a problem. I have only been drunk once in my lifetime; I never took off from work because of drunkness. I never stayed away from home for 1 to 2 days because I was drinking. I can't say the same for crack cocaine; that's a different animal. A lot of my setbacks, my therapist explained, were the fact that I was drinking; she said it always led me back to using. Brenda heard the therapist make this statement. She would hold it over my head whenever she saw me drinking or having a glass of wine at dinner. Brenda asked me, "Why do you think that just because your day is going badly, using drugs or drinking will make it better? Because someone pissed you off, you decide to show them; why do you feel you have the right to mess up someones' day? Why do you feel you can stop just when you get ready? Jimmy, you need some help; your way of thinking is so warped, and whatever you are doing is not working. You need professional help, and if you don't get it, there will be more terrible days ahead..." And she was right.

As my days become ordinary, ordinary to me, that's a day without the hassle of using. Not having to lie about where I have been or money I may have spent. I often think about Connie. Connie said God has a plan for all of us and that we were special. She said we may not know what the plan is, but it will be revealed in due time. God's time. In the meantime, we should live our lives to the fullest. God does not want our life to be burdened with drugs and alcohol; We should live each day of our life like it's a gift from God. Most of my days are spent trying to stay focused. I read my big book and the bible from time to time. Reading always put me to sleep, but I would manage to get a little reading in. I try to keep myself busy, and Brenda normally keeps me busy with a 'honey-do" list. I think about my mother who raised me and how she would toil in her garden and her flower beds, and she would go fishing every chance she got. I remember digging worms as a child just so she could go fishing—anything to keep me from working in the garden. I realize now how much those things meant to her. It was rewarding to her; it gave her some sort of peace of mind and a feeling of accomplishment. That's why I stay busy with a positive attitude.

Well, today is the day I have been working towards. Today is the day I go back to work. I don't feel nervous about it anymore. Whatever my co-worker's responses are, I will have to overcome them; they have their opinions, and that's their right. One thing is for sure: I will not be alone; God will be with me like he has always been. God will always do his part. Will I do mine? God has brought me through all the storms that I put myself in, storms that I could have, and should have, and wished I would have avoided. I just have to make sure my ship continues to sail smoothly; after all, I am the captain. It's Sunday; whoa, let me back up to Saturday because it's been an interesting weekend so far. Last night, I went to my NA meeting on Saturday night. The topic was about rituals that we, as addicts, sometimes go through when we use.

I never believed I went through any type of ritual or any other ceremonial act. But I did have a distinct pattern that I always followed, and my wife knew it every time. The pattern was always the same. She knew that if she went out of town, I would use it, and that she was 90 percent correct. I was gone for a day or two, and on that, she was 100 percent correct. And I told the same old lies; on that, she was 100 percent correct. No matter how I tried to change my habits, the results were the same. I changed my patterns. I started attending church more and became more involved in my NA meeting. If I went to the grocery store, I would always carry one of the kids with me so I would have a witness; if I went by myself, I would always give a specific time when I would be back. That was torture, I felt less than a responsible person, which is the sign of a person who can not be trusted. Nobody said I was right or wrong; that was what I, as an addict, had to do to get my trust back, and this was the way I felt about it. No one wants to be in any type of relationship where there is no trust.

They say, "Go to 90 meetings in 90 days." The purpose of this is to change your habits. Start new positive patterns; recovery is about change. I can't stress this enough.

I went to church this morning. Today was Mother's Day. They did a special service for mothers. It was good to be at church and be a part of the service. Got a call from Jim T today. It was good to hear from him. Jim was with me at Highland Ridge. I asked how he was doing, and he said he was kind of down. I asked why. He said, "Do you remember the kid with the wild hair?" I said yes, his name is Steve, and he carried me out to lunch one day. He told me that Steve was shot and killed by the police earlier today at his father-in-law's house. Steve lived in Utah, where Jim lived. I was totally shocked. My first response was, "What the hell is going on?" First Trent, now Steve. Trent had taken an overdose a couple of months ago. Jim went on to give me details, which I vaguely heard.

I was thinking to myself, what a waste of life. Steve was not on crack cocaine, nor was he an alcoholic; his issue was opioids, that's what most of the people that was in rehab had issues with, opioids. Steve was a young man who, besides the opioids issue, seemed to have so much to live for. I remember the first time I saw him—kind of a flashy dresser, tall and lanky with a happy-go-lucky lifestyle. A fun person to be around, but I am sure he got a little wild when he was doped up. In spite of his flaws, the young man had a lot going on for himself. He had his own little business. He sold cell phones, a beautiful wife, and kids, so much to live for. In fact, he and I went to dinner on the Friday before I came home. We talked about the pressures drugs had put on our lives. Even though there was a big difference in our age, we shared a common bond as addicts. Steve was a good young man who wanted to have fun. He had some of the ingredients for success and a recipe for failure with his drug use; he always seemed like he was hanging on by a thread. He was naturally hyper. We shared a few war stories and a few laughs.

I tried to enlighten him on some positive things I had learned in life and hoped that he would apply them to help him get through the program. One of the main things I tried to instill in him was to stay in the program. That was a tough one since he was paying his own way. He could leave at any time he wanted to. I commended him for seeking help on his own. I told him to try to grow from his mistakes. Growing from your mistakes is a vital part of an addict's recovery. The one thing that I did learn from my first rehab was the fact that I had a problem. There was no denying that fact, but I did. I explained to him that I wanted to protect my habit. I did not want it taken away, but the thought of me having a drug habit stayed in mind, kinda like the first hit of crack cocaine stayed in my mind. When I had my first hit, it was nearly a year before I did it again, but that first time, the seed had been planted. It stayed in the back of my brain cells for some purpose, and that purpose was that someday I would do something about it. I told him now I realize I have a problem with crack, and I am going to do all I can to make my life better. I am here because I choose to be; you, Steve, are here because you need to be. Your life is getting out of control. I mentioned to him that quitting or breaking habits is not an easy thing to accomplish. Sometimes, help is needed, and there are some who go cold turkey. I quit cigarettes cold turkey, and yes, I will get the urge from time to time to smoke again, but I make it; that's where my strength comes from, and the rewards are so great. All I wanted Steve to do was give himself a chance. A chance to live. Drugs and alcohol take away that chance if you allow it. It shortens your days, and it does nothing but cause problems. My being clean and sober today lets me know I am doing something right.

Sunday night, time to go back to work. I work the 3rd shift, graveyard, and I love it. After the event that took place today concerning Steve, going back to work is a welcome break. I'm getting a little worked up, but I am okay.

I made it to work ahead of schedule. I was welcomed back with open arms, or at least it seemed that way. No one gave me the impression I had anything to be afraid of or ashamed of, but I could also tell no one wanted to address the issues of where I had been for the past nearly four months. I am sure rumors were circulating concerning my whereabouts. I found myself trying to explain things that did not need explaining. My whereabouts were not really their concern. No need to explain things that they would probably not understand anyway. I made it through the night okay, as well as the other couple of nights. It seemed like I was beginning to settle back into the groove of things. God, thank you; I am beginning to feel whole again. All of a sudden, everything seemed short-lived; all of the warm greetings were over, and I had stepped into my role as a supervisor, giving out jobs and dealing with the ordinary tasks that go along with the job. As the week went on, I found myself making mistakes, writing down wrong numbers on my paperwork, and it seemed my coworkers were catching every mistake. I was starting to overplay things in my mind, but in reality, all I was doing was making honest mistakes with my paperwork. My mind was looking for the worst-case scenario. Maybe I was getting a little paranoid. I could feel the drops of sweat coming from under my armpits. There was one particular time I just went for a walk. I found myself starting over when I made a mistake on my paperwork. I was trying to be perfect; It seemed all eyes were on me; even at home with family, my wife would question me like a child on the first day of school. I made it through the week and was glad to see my off days. In spite of it all, I am very glad and thankful that I have a job. I know time will ease some of the pain and self-pity I still carry concerning myself and my life. But for now, I thank God for giving me strength and wisdom to be part of an ever-changing universe. I don't worry about fitting in; I fit in right where I belong in God's plan. I take it one day at a time, and I treasure every minute of it.

I am coming up on 4 months of sobriety and clean time. I have been asked to chair meetings at the NA meetings that I attend. I remember back at Highland Ridge in Utah, we had to attend meetings, and it was part of our treatment. I was amazed at how the meetings were conducted. Little did I know they had a format that they used, but it was something that I wanted to do. Now I get the chance to give back, so be careful what you ask for. I felt this was a good opportunity for me to use some of my people skills. I was nervous my first time. Who wouldn't be? I was glad when it was over. It was a promise I had fulfilled; even though it was small in stature, it meant a lot to me.

Several weeks have gone by; I am really getting back to the flow of doing things in my life that have meaning and purpose. As I was leaving work this particular morning, I noticed all the people going fishing. Some had bass boats, and some had flat-bottom boats.The bait shops that I passed on the way home and the parking lots were full. Many times when I was using, there were times when I wished I could have gone fishing. My drug use had taken that joy away. When I was a child, my mother would always take me fishing. She seems to get so much peace and joy from fishing. So with that in mind, I started planning myself a fishing trip. I still had my flat-bottom boat, and I finally got my bass boat sold. I spent most of the money catching up on past due bills. I had yet to receive my first paycheck after returning to work. That's a 30-day process, so I have to manage my money accordingly. It had been over a year since I had gone fishing. I was eager to get back to some of the things I had been doing, such as fishing and shooting pool. My wife and I would spend a lot of quality time on the lake fishing, well, let's say I was fishing; she was sunbathing, and we had fun. But this time it was going to be me and the lake. I had managed to put back a hundred-dollar bill for really hard times during this recovery period. To tell the truth, things were not going as planned. Somehow, the hundred-dollar bill I thought I had saved, I could not find it. I hid it in one of my hiding places, at least that is what I thought. Mmmm... I always had a habit of hiding money, but I normally remember where to go back and find it. Like I said earlier, you can't hide money from yourself, but you might forget where you put it. I looked everywhere. I didn't want her to think anything to the contrary. I did not need any suspicion thrown my way. I was already feeling guilty about holding money back, especially since finances were in a crunch. I told my wife about the money; she seemed rather calm about the situation. She told me that this was not the first time I had done this. She said, "With everything on your mind, you just forgot where you put it; you will find it." With every plan, there should always be a backup. That's right, plan B. I had saved some money by not buying cigarettes for myself, but she was still smoking, and you don't want to be around her when she doesn't have her cigarettes. It had been about 5 months since I had smoked a cigarette. I was doing good with my addictions. The Items I needed for the trip came to bout 80 dollars. I needed a battery for the boat, a fishing bait, a fishing license, soft drinks and snacks. I also figured out a new rod. You might think that with all my purchases, this was my very first time fishing. But as I mentioned, it had been a while. The excitement was building up. So I took my list of things I needed and headed to Walmart. I really had to watch my spending; fishing can get pricy, so stick to the list. I walked the aisles at Walmart, found all the items I needed, checked out, and headed back home. As I was getting out of my SUV at home, somehow, I had managed to break the tip off my rod. I could hardly believe what had just happened to me, and it quickly dawned on me that I had probably thrown my receipt away while cleaning out my SUV at the car wash. I carried the items I had inside the house. But I figured taking it back would not be a problem. Back to Walmart, I go. I went to the area where I had checked out, hoping the same clerk who checked me out was still working the register. I was wrong. A different clerk was at the register. I could feel that the situation was going to turn sour. I cautiously approached the clerk and told her my situation. She said, I am sorry, but I can not exchange the item unless you have a receipt. I told her that I had accidentally thrown my receipt away and that I had been in earlier and bought the rod. She asked my name, and I told her. She did some cross-referencing with the SKU number on the rod, and it showed it had been sold earlier that day. She told me to go and find another rod. I thought to myself, "Well, that was easy." I proceeded to get another fishing rod, but before I could get back, she had already started the exchange paperwork. She said all I need is to see your driver's license or some form of ID. She stated that was the only way she could make the exchange. That's when I realized I had left my driver's license at home. I told her that I had bought my fishing license earlier. She stated, "How did you buy your fishing license without an ID?" I stated I had my wallet, then I just left it at home. All of a sudden, it dawn on me that this was going nowhere with this clerk, and I was beginning to get a little upset... pissed off is a better way to describe it

As I raised my head to the ceiling with that look of disgust on my face, I quickly closed my eyes and started thinking about the trip I would have to make to go home and get my wallet; this would take a good hour with traffic and all. I lowered my head slowly, releasing the tension that had built up. I looked her right in the eyes and said those famous words from the movie *Terminator*: I'll be back. She gave me a slight grin and told me she was sorry. As I left the store, I asked myself, whose fault is this? There was no need to upset the clerk at the register, who was doing her job. I could have left there, blaming her and ruining her day, plus upsetting myself. I found in rehab that people seem to blame other people for their bad habits, whether it's alcohol, drugs, food, smoking, or whatever they are addicted to. Not wanting to accept responsibility, we point the finger at someone else; never do we point our finger at the person in the mirror. I feel that, as an addict, I sometimes blame others for my mistakes. Nobody put a gun to my head and made me do anything I didn't want to do, just some of my character defects, I suppose.

I got the fishing rod situation all taken care of, got all my stuff, and I am ready to go fishing. I felt so good, I invited my neighbor across the street. He had often told me he wanted to go fishing with me sometime. I told him I wanted to leave at about 5 am so we could get to the lake at about dawn. So that evening, I gathered all my stuff, gassed up my boat and SUV, and bought worms. I was ready for the Saturday morning fishing trip. Things did not start too well. I got up late, at 5:45 a.m. I really thought I had set my alarm for 5:00 a.m., but I guess I did not.

No big deal; things will be okay. Little did I know that by getting up late, the tone for the day had been set. My neighbor and I stopped at a local bait shop that morning to get him some fish bait and snacks. As we were pulling away from the bait shop, I realized I had left my fishing bait at home. I am trying to hold my head up because I am determined to go fishing today. So, instead of going back home, which would have taken another 30 minutes, I went back to the bait shop and bought more fishing bait. As I was going back into the bait shop, I walked around the end of the boat; I just happened to look down, and guess what? I noticed the tags on my boat had expired. I do not believe this, I said to myself. That's when I started shouting out those four-letter ungodly words with those ungodly meanings. The ones that began with S and the other one began with F. I kept walking from the bait shop, cussing all the way to the counter. I was not directing my words at anyone but myself. This was beginning to get to me a little, and it seemed it started yesterday with the fishing rod. I made my purchase, came out of the store, got into my SUV, and drove off like everything was ok. Praying I don't get stopped by the police.

We made it to the lake, but not as early as I had planned. Once we arrived, we realized we were the only ones there; to me, this was not a good sign that we were going to have a good fishing day. Judging from the surroundings, nobody had fished in this area for quite some time. This used to be one of my favorite fishing spots. I found it hard to believe no one was there; it was a beautiful day for fishing. We finally launched my little flat-bottom fishing boat, and after cranking on it for about 10 minutes, it finally cranked up, and off we went. It did not get very far from the bank, and the boat died. I jerked on the boat a few more pulls, cranked up, and off we went again. Well, what else can go wrong? Please read on; this was just the beginning. It would run and stop; this process went on until we made it to the other side of the lake. In spite of all the cranking and stopping and restarting and the no-shows on the lake, none of this was going to dampen my spirit for fishing. I had thought about this spot when I was in the treatment program. My stepson, who is now in the Navy, and I used to fish at this spot quite often. He and I spent a lot of quality time fishing this lake. For a kid, he was a pretty good fisherman. He would always beat me at bass fishing. I love that kid. Even though my neighbor and I faced a few setbacks, we wandered around until we finally found a place to anchor and cast our lines. I cast to a spot that looked picture-perfect, right under a branch that was barely touching the water. No sooner had my cork hit the water than my cork went under. Something had it and gone. I jerked so hard that the backward momentum broke my boat seat.

I tried correcting myself so that I would not fall out of the boat; in doing so, I created a snowball effect. I fell backward, broke the tip off my rod, and rolled my right foot to kick over the cricket bucket. There were crickets crawling all over the bottom of the boat, somehow I kicked the bag of snacks out of the boat, turn over the minnow bucket which we did not realize until about 30 minutes later which was to late because all the minnows had died, yes every last one, as far as the bite I had whatever it was managed to get me hung up and I ended up striping the gears on my reel the only good rod and reel I had left. I guess you can say my fishing trip was really sucking, to put it mildly. But for the next hour or so, we managed to catch a few fish. Thank God I had brought my crappie pole.

Now I look back at this and see how enjoyable it was, and just being there was a blessing. My worst day fishing was a whole lot better than my best day drugging. If you are not an addict, you might not understand that statement. The fishing adventure is the kind of adventure that I can look back on and laugh about, compared to looking back on the days I used to make people around me feel miserable. I will always remember that trip, and so will my neighbor, Gary. I will cherish it, it had a positive effect, and I made it through that day without using.

As life goes on, my daily routines have changed, and they have changed for the better. I made some simple changes in my life. I changed my music from pop to jazz, which had become more relaxing, especially in my game room. It fills my mind with a feeling of tranquility; it allows me to breathe. Pop music had become a stark reminder of my using days. These were songs that I listened to during my hunt for crack cocaine, not by choice; they always seemed to be playing. In fact, one CD in particular was stuck in my CD player. It was Bobby Brown... "Every little step I take..." It's now over 20 years later, I hate that song. I shoot pool with my best friend, who has that song recorded. I tell him, Ron, I hate that song, that song has left me scarred. I go on to tell him why. The year is the early summer of 2003; my heart is filled with excitement because I am looking forward to helping coach my grandson Drake's Little League baseball team.

I made a promise to him, and I try to keep my promises. I helped coach a few years ago. It's fun if you allow it to be, plus you are giving back, and it occupies your mind and time. I am still going to my NA meeting twice a week. Going to these meetings allows me to vent some of my frustrations. It also gives me the opportunity to share and listen to others. I enjoy listening to other people talk about the program and how it has transformed their lives. They said the key was to be true to yourself, the one person you can not fool. Sometimes, you just want someone to listen. They can't solve your problems; only you can do that, whether you are an addict or not. You have to make the choice to do the right thing. Life deals with choices, and choices have consequences; even God gives you a choice. It's a good feeling to see people being honest and caring. People who are concerned about your state of mind and well-being. I know my wife was concerned, but being concerned alone won't cut it. I know she wanted me to overcome my addiction. She would always give me words of encouragement, she would not try to tear me down too much, but there were times when she would really explode on me, and sometimes that made it worse.

I am eagerly waiting for July 2003; that's when I began my quest for the Class B State Pool Championship. If I don't win it this year, I will sit down and think seriously about continuing to play pool on the pool circuit. I know sooner or later, it's going to cause a problem with Brenda and me. I don't want to cause any problems with it interfering with my sobriety. Sometimes, pool tournaments are held in establishments where alcohol is sold. It's going to be up to me to make a choice.

There have been no drastic negative changes in my life after over four months of clean time. I am catching up on my bills; there are always little setbacks, but that's life. I deal with them the best I can and move on. I feel God is taking care of my needs; I am enjoying my clean time.

I woke up this past Sunday morning and was doing some channel surfing on my television when I came across Minister Stanley Clark talking about how the devil fires missiles at us. He talked about how the Devil gets you to submit to his will by seducing your mind with ungodly thoughts. I was comparing that to my addiction. They say the addiction never rests, neither does the Devil. The addiction is always there, and so is the Devil. The addiction is tricky and cunning, so is the Devil. In NA, they have this chant that goes like this... "Don't do it; it's a trick." I can't count how many times I said to myself... "Don't do it; it's a trick." I never listened to myself. The addiction, just like the Devil, always keeps me hanging. I would tell myself, "Just 20 dollars worth is all I am going to do." Brothers and sisters, it doesn't work like that. So many times, I set myself up for the fall, and fall I did. Falling into the trap. It's such a relief to know that God has no traps, God has no tricks up his sleeves; in my addiction, there are always battles of good and evil, even today, some 20 years later. God allows you to make that choice; sometimes, that choice can be fatal. In my addiction, I was fighting such a battle. I thank God for the things that were instilled in me in my childhood by my parents, who raised me. I was raised the old-fashioned way: fear. If you screwed up, you got your but whipped. That was fear. They instilled in me right from wrong respect for yourself and respect for your elders. They put a solid foundation in my mind. It was simple; it's called right and wrong. A foundation that the Devil could not tear down. Storms may come against you, your ship will get tossed in the sea of ungodliness, but fear kept me bound to my foundation. Even in the midst of insanity, I remember what my foundation was about. I could hear my mother's voice telling me to stay out of trouble, not run with bad company, go to church, and honor my mother and father. That's what my foundation was built on. Somewhere in my adult life, I lost some of that. There was a price to pay, and I am paying it today. I allowed my will instead of God's will to guide me. It carried me places that I should not have gone, mentally and physically. The use of drugs really tore me down spiritually.Please, don't get me wrong about the things I say. I am not into any type of devil-worshipping or anything of that nature, but doing crack cocaine made me look at myself in a different light. I felt I was being controlled, and I was. The addition had its grip on me. The more I tried to resist, the deeper I sank. I am sure you have heard of people killing their loved ones, and you hear about them being high on crack. I say they were not high on crack, but instead they were feeding the craving of the addiction of crack cocaine, needing a hit, wanting to get high, that's what made us feel normal. The stupid stuff some people did for crack is mind-blowing. Oh, I did some stupid stuff myself, but I am not here to talk about my stupidity. I have talked about it enough. If you have read up until now, I am sure you see that my stupidity was obvious. Instead, it's the acceptance of things I had to do. I had to make a change. I thank God for sparing me the guilt and total embarrassment that some people went through. When you put your job, your family, your friends, and your belief in your God in that bullseye, you can't do anything but fall. I am here to tell you, God and the people he put in my life kept me from falling rock bottom, but I sure stumbled a lot. My stumbling really caused me to take a reality check on my life. You tell yourself I would never do that, I would never rob or kill someone for drugs. I would be willing to bet the same people who killed or robbed probably made that same statement. I stole from the church. Remember, stealing is stealing, no matter how you look at it. I remember seeing this documentary on crack cocaine use; it was back in the 80s. Crack cocaine was just beginning to come on the scene down south. This documentary showed the effect that crack cocaine had on the inner cities like Chicago and Detroit. It stated it was a highly addictive drug. As I sat and watched, I said to myself, "No way, no way would I destroy myself that way; they've got to be crazy." Well, look who's crazy. Never say what you won't do. When you get under the influence, there is no telling where the influence will lead you. Even when I was not under the influence of the crack, I found myself breaking the law. I had hot checks all over the city. I went to court for several hot checks. In fact, I had about 1500 dollars in hot check penalties and fines. I went before one judge who told me if I wrote one more hot check and it appeared before him, he was going to do his best to send me to the penitentiary. I went home and tore up my checkbooks. I don't write checks today. He ain't got to worry about me. I don't write checks today, and I don't take checks. I learned my lesson from that judge. He meant business. To be fair and honest, this was years before my marriage. I am sure my story is pale in comparison to some, because I heard stories that made my head spin. That's why I don't like war stories. The point that I am trying to convey is the fact that my situation was beginning to escalate. If it wasn't for the grace of God, I might have made the evening news also.

Today is Saturday, May 30, 2003, four months clean and sober. Four months of change due to positive thinking and action. I attend the meetings I am supposed to attend, and I share my experiences with others. I let them know that getting off drugs does not guarantee life, but it does make a life possible that you can believe in. I spend less time reflecting on days gone by, and I don't spend a lot of time trying to look into the future; one day at a time is all I can deal with. I'm still goal-oriented, but if I don't reach certain plateaus, it does not mean that I am a failure. It only means I didn't reach a certain goal. I accept that and move on.

About three weeks ago, a guy I knew as a friend died of a heart attack. He was 47 years old. A good guy, no drugs that I knew of. The news of this really saddened me; he was what I called an "old school" friend from back in the day. What caused his death in the prime of his life? He smoked cigarettes; he loved drinking his Crown Royal. These are some of the things I can only assume. He was overweight, loved to drink his Crown, did not get enough exercise, and who knows what else was going on in his life. Sitting and thinking about this made me realize I was taking my life for granted, and for what? It's a shame how we cut our lives short by abusing our bodies and minds. People will probably say it was his time to die. I say only because it was made that way, and this is just my opinion. The Bible states, in so many words, that we all have an appointed time to come and an appointed time to leave. But you can ruin your life with the lifestyle you live. And drugs and alcohol play no part. It depends on your life or your occupation; you could be working a dangerous job, and you get what I'm talking about. I believe that if you continue to do things that are harmful to the body, you are punching your death clock. Even the body gives off warning signs. Do we listen? Do we take heed?

I smoked so much crack on one particular binge that my whole body went into cramps. I crammed so hard I could barely hold the lighter to light the cracked pipe... Did I stop?... Hell, naw!! That's the insanity; getting high was more important than life, it seemed. I have seen a user take one hit, and their whole face becomes deformed.

Their speech becomes slurred, and their mouth starts twitching. Now, if those aren't warning signs, I don't know what warning signs are. Some just look at this as being the side effects of the drugs, and I say... Yeah. Cancer is the side effect of smoking, and we all know cancer kills. Honesty speaking, it did not bother me all that much when I was using, that I could lose my life, especially in my early stages of using. My theory was always... It won't happen to me... I don't know why I felt invincible. Like I said before, I was more concerned about the police than I was about dying. Life has its own set of rules. As an addict, I keep adding to them, making life more complicated. I boost it up with drugs and alcohol, trying to give it that little kick, adding a little spike to the punch. Normal just isn't good enough anymore. I truly believe God does not want his children to suffer; all the misery that I dealt with, I brought it on myself and sometimes others.

All the meetings that I have attended talk about sharing and giving back. They also say recovery involves action. You cannot just sit around waiting for things to happen to you. You must put what little knowledge you have into action. I can't think of a better way to give back than by chairing and sharing. Chairing seems to give a sense of helping; sometimes, listening to someone may not help you, but it could help the person who is talking to you. I know there were times I just wanted to talk with someone about how bad I felt after someone had been affected by my actions. "By giving back, you are paying for your raising," as my mother would say.

You are being taught how to live life on life's terms, not yours. I look forward to my meetings; I look forward to the fellowship among my members. I have not attended a meeting yet, from which I have not benefited. By sharing, I will be giving something back, like my experience of what the program has done for me in my short period of recovery. I am sure you will have a feeling of happiness by sharing your knowledge of what you have learned about something. I know the main thing I learned was I had a problem and was in denial, like many others who first come into the rehab program, and I will go as far as to say that some probably leave still in denial. To me, that means you were not ready for rehab.

Coming upon six months of clean time, my life is filled with a lot of clarity. I am able to see things with a clearer view. Yes, some days are better than others. Some days I get a little angry and frustrated. I realize anger is an emotion that I should handle without trying to direct it at others. People can be so mean to one another simply because they are having a bad day. I mostly get upset over personal matters, like things I have done to myself. I usually find myself a quiet place and deal with it. Brenda, I feel sometimes she tries to shut off my anger, and she also takes it as a sign of me wanting to use. I can feel that type of vibe coming from her. I am being honest, I still have cravings, but I am learning how to deal with them. I treat my cravings as if they are growing pains. I admit I am not good at talking things out all the time, and it's also good sometimes to keep things under wraps. You don't want to go adding fuel to a volatile situation. I feel there are certain issues in my life that I have the right to get emotionally upset about, while Brenda seems to think she can solve all my little anger issues. She had a tendency to consume herself with my issues when I went to NA meetings. It had gotten to the point where I invited her not to go a time or two. It was really causing problems. I also understood her point of view; after all, my drug usage had an effect on her life as well. She spent a lot of energy trying to protect me. Covering for me when I did not go to work. Lying to the children about me having to work overtime, not knowing what's going on with me when I am gone for a day or two. It takes a special kind of person to deal with this. But I can see it's taking its toll on her as a person and as my wife. The guilt that I carry now is about the pain she went through.

I have said to her a time or two, "I don't know if I could have done what you are doing." Sometimes, she does overreact to my emotions. She told me she was trying to protect what little feelings she had left. I know she is emotionally drained; she not only has to contend with her mother's ailing health, which is a handful in itself. I try to reassure her by working my program and by giving an account of where I am and where I will be. She and I are spending more time together. I am not trying to atone for the lost time because I cannot change what I have done; I can only work to make sure it doesn't happen again.

Talked to Ded F., a friend I met back at Highland Ridge. We had not talked since I left the treatment center nearly seven months ago. I was glad to hear from her; she told me she was slowly getting the pieces of her life back together. She said she had spent three months in a halfway house in California. We talked about the tragedy that had happened with Trent G. and Steve. We talked about the unity that the group had and about how much we meant to each other. Deb and I had some really intense conversations back at the treatment center. We arrived at about the same time. I remember the first time I saw her, she had on that blue denim overall outfit. You could see sadness all over her face; she looked like she had been on her last binge last night. She looked as if she had the weight of the world on her shoulders; it seemed her life was filled with extra baggage. Baggage she doesn't want to let go of or feels she can't release. Letting go is a healing process. It's called surrender; in wrestling, it's referred to as tapping out or giving up. You are not going to beat it by continuing to wrestle with it. If a poll were taken, Deb would have been the most loved. She was sweet and soft-spoken; it was good to hear from her. I believe she found that serenity is something we all seek in our lives, whether you are an addict or not. I told her about he people I had talked with, and everyone seemed to be doing ok. I told her I had talked to Jim T a few days ago. It was a pleasure to talk with him. Deb and I said our goodbyes and promised to keep in touch. Conversations like that make my day, knowing someone I care about, whose life has been in turmoil, has made a positive change.

My church attendance has fallen off somewhat. I have missed a couple of Sundays, but I am still strong in my NA meetings. I have not picked up any bad habits. Eight months since I have smoked a cigarette, I feel good about that. I spend some of my spare time going to the Wellness Center. Sometimes, Brenda goes with me. I go there about twice a week. I am trying to get rid of some of the extra pounds I have picked up over the winter months. Brenda's cooking and my clean living have really made a difference in the past several months. I have taken my second drug screening at the job in less than 5 weeks. The satisfaction of not having to worry about passing a drug screening is so comforting. As I look back at all the things I burden myself with, not to mention others, it's amazing that I survived. All the praise and glory go to God. I praise myself for being able to step into Life. My life has become stable since I quit using both crack cocaine and cigarettes.

Catching up is a very hard thing to do, but I am getting there. My stepson will be coming home from the Navy soon. He has been overseas doing his tour of military duty in the Iraq War. I really made a mess of his last visit. I hope to make up for it this time when he comes home; I owe him a fishing trip and a big apology.

One person, along with Brenda, asked me in an NA meeting what makes this time going to a treatment center any different from the times before. This was the question that was asked of me back in February of 2003, the month I went to the Rehab center in Utah. I had been to rehab twice before she expressed her doubts. When Brenda asked me, all I could do was look her in the eyes and try to walk away. I really had no answer at the moment she asked me, but after thinking for a minute, I finally told her. I said that the first time I went, I did not want to quit. I was merely going into treatment just for protection, protection for my job, and protection for myself. I said, "To be honest, my sister intervened. I really found no joy in what was happening in my life, but I was bound and determined to protect my addiction." My first stay at a treatment center was a disaster. I didn't gain anything from the program, not due to the program itself, but because I didn't invest any effort into it; I didn't apply myself. I was not the least bit interested in quitting. My party was just getting started, and I was mad at my sister because she intervened. My oldest sister, Birthola, had been like my guardian angel all my life. I remember her telling me the story of our sister Joyce setting the house on fire, how her being a baby herself got me and my other sister out of the house. Bert, as I call her, was about 6 years old, Joyce was about 4 years old, and I was about 2 years old. My biological mother was alive during this time period. She also told me about the time I crawled out of the house without anyone knowing and was playing in the middle of the road, an old country dirt road. She said she barely got me out before a big truck came along. She told me she always felt compelled to protect me, and she would do it until the day she dies or I die. I have always thanked her for coming to my rescue. Back in 1991, a couple of months after my father's death, my life was a wreck. I was blind and did not want to see it. I was missing work at an unbelievable pace. I had lost weight, I had used all the holes in my belt, and it seemed every day I was punching a new hole in my belt just to get my pants to stay up. The crack cocaine was drying me up. I remember one of my bosses asking me what type of diet I was on... Now that I look back, it was a crack diet... I told him that sardines and rice will make you lose weight really fast. I also put my weight loss on my depression, of losing my father. What a sad excuse that was, but anything to throw people off track of my usage. Countless times, I would leave work early just to go use. My lifestyle was wide open, but to me, I was having the time of my life. Even at the age of 40, I was so disillusioned, with no awareness of fear. My main objective every day was to get high. I had just purchased a new vehicle back in 1991. I had had it for nearly 4 months and had not made a payment. It was totally insane to ride around in a new car with no tags. smoking dope. I know it sounds unreal but my dumb ass did it. Back then, I was so unappreciative of my sister, but because of her intervention and a little trickery, she did her part as far as getting me into the Treatment Program. Going into the Treatment center for the first time, I had no idea what to expect. The only thing I knew was the fact that I did not want to be there. I am reminded of the younger group at Highland Ridge, the ones I talked with did not want to be there. Some were court-ordered, some because of their job, some because the parents sent them there, marriage, the list goes on and on. It was difficult for some to be submissive. They were more concerned with what was going on outside than they were with the inside of the treatment program. My resistance to the program was built up because of my unwillingness to give the program a try, and besides, I was in denial. It was a 40-day program. If the treatment center had adhered to its rules, I would have been kicked out in the 2nd week. I got a weekend pass on a Friday, but I was supposed to return on Sunday. Instead, I returned on Tuesday. Flunked my reentry screening, but I wisely blamed it on them. I told them you allowed me to leave with someone who had been in ten treatment programs. I was a rookie, he was a veteran. I will never forget his name; his name was Todd. I haven't seen him since that day, and guess what? I don't want to see him. I promised them I would be more responsive, and they allowed me to stay. From that point on, I began to absorb some of the program. After I got out of the program and went back to work about a week later... I relapsed. That's when my ten-year struggle for recovery really began.

My second time going to a Treatment center, I explained, "I did it from the fear of losing my job. I used this opportunity as a get out of jail free card. I was learning the loopholes of the Treatment program with my job." This time, the Treatment center was my refuge. I only stayed five days, but those five days really opened my eyes more than the 40-day stay. I agreed to go to aftercare programs and attend AA meetings; they granted me an early release. For a while there, I thought I was really going to do well. It was my intention anyway. I attended a few AA meetings. It lasted about 6 months before I relapsed. I found myself going on binges every three or four months. To me, this period was the worst because my attitude about using was changing.

Deep down inside, I wanted to quit more than ever. I could feel the changes my life was going through, but by now, the hole I had dug had gotten bigger. The addiction had dug itself deeper into my veins. Brenda saw all the warning signs. I continued to stay in denial. I did not want to give up my freedom to drink a beer or have a glass of wine at dinner or at any given time. I would argue with Brenda until I got my way, and every time I did it my way, my life would go the other way. I remember one incident when I got off work, stopped at a crack house, and bought a twenty-dollar rock.

I told myself that was all I was going to spend. Well, that was all I spent the first time. But within eight hours, I had spent over three hundred dollars. As I sat and came down off my high, reality began to start kicking in, reminding me of what I had done. I began to fear the usual, and that usual is facing Brenda and the rest of the family. How was I going to explain this? Somehow, I always feared what I did not have to fear when it comes to this matter. She already knew what was going on, I mean, my God, I have not been home since I got off from work. She knew what my patterns were. So what do I do? As I continued to sit there, like this would make my problem disappear, it had never worked before, so why would it now? The sun had gone down, and I was nearly broke with a half tank of gas. Too afraid to go home, not enough money to get high, getting high would ease the pain. I rode around for hours. I finally ended up calling a friend who was also a fellow worker, Rudy. It was about 11 pm or so, I told him my situation, and I needed his help.

I wanted him to take me to the Treatment center, and without hesitation, he carried me. I trust that God places people in our lives, yet the mystery of their purpose remains unexplained. People try, and everyone has their opinion. Once we arrived, I checked myself in. It was quite embarrassing to me because this was the same Treatment Center I went to the first time. I remember telling them I won't be back... Well, that's not the first time I have lied, and I am sure it won't be my last. Once I got settled in, I called Brenda and told her where I was. She took the situation quite lightly, and she asked her usual questions. But this time, she did no cussing, no name-calling, no yelling. I was really thrown off track by her reactions. Never before had she ever acted this calm. She did go on to tell me how she felt about the situation and gave me credit for my efforts in trying to get off the drugs. Once again, I had used the system to my advantage. I was only there for about 48 hours. Since I checked myself in, I could check myself out. I didn't miss any days from work because it happened on my off days. All I basically did was get some good rest. This short stint in the treatment center really planted a seed in my mind. But did I stop? The answer is no... I have managed to binge less and less, if that's any consolation at all, and it's not... So, back to the original question, why is this TIME so different?

The answer is quite simple... I am tired, I am nearly 50 years old, and I am going through these types of life changes. It's like a slave who wants his freedom. I am a slave to this addiction. The only way to defeat it is to surrender. Drop the denial. It's not good to live a life where you are being controlled, no matter what those controlling factors may be. Drugs give you a false sense of control.

You hear people in the group meeting talking about making amends. Amends is part of the 12-step program. That reminds me of when Seth came home. He and I sat and had a long conversation. He told me about how proud he was of me due to the fact that I was getting my life back together. I felt he always respected me for the type of person he believed I was inside, not the person who made some bad choices. He currently re-enlisted in the military; he has a bright future ahead. I always wish him the best. By having this conversation with him, I really hope I made amends with Seth by explaining to him how sorry I was about the things that happened between us and what I had put the family through, and I would do all within my power to keep it from happening again.

As far as my job is concerned, I have not worked since August 2003. I am currently off work due to a personal injury. I do not have to go through drug screening since I am off from work. I am sure that as soon as I am able to go back to work, I will be put back in the system. Being off from work created a few challenges for me. It meant I had more time on my hands. The saying goes, "An idle mind is the devil's workshop." I keep myself as busy as possible. I have limitations on what I can do around home, due to my illness. I have increased my meetings to 3 per week. I try to attend church every Sunday. On that, I failed; I attended the best I could. I often pick up my grandson Drake from school. By not working, I get plenty of rest at night. When I was working, I worked the third shift, but my sleeping at night really made a difference as far as rest is concerned. It makes a difference in how I feel the next day, rested. Brenda and I spend more time talking. We occasionally go fishing in our little flat-bottom boat, and we miss the old bass boat. We, as a family, had a lot of good times out on the water with the bass boat, especially being out on the water during the 4th of July fireworks. Brenda tells me from time to time that she can see the change in my patterns and attitude. She did admit she thought I would do this for a while and quit. That was my old pattern. Speaking of quitting, I have tried talking to her about her smoking cigarettes. She overwhelms herself with smoking. I quit, believe it or not... cold turkey... People have asked me... "How do you quit, and your wife still smokes?" I was reluctant to tell them the real reason, which was that smoking triggered my craving for crack.

Additionally, a cigarette lighter and crack went hand in hand for me. I learned triggers and buzzwords from my first rehab. So I did learn something from the program.

On January 19, 2004, Brenda had a mild heart attack. She had a heart attack back in 1992, the year we got married. She was young and very active then, played tennis, attended her children's Little League games, swam, and had fun times with her friends. This was a major surgery for someone her age. Brenda was a fighter; she was strong. But she would not put those cigarettes down. This surgery that she was having now was minor. This does not take away from the danger of having any type of surgery. Her heart specialist warned her to quit smoking. Just like millions of people who smoke, let's be real here: they are addicted. They may not be missing any days from work or going on binges; they will tell a lie or two about their smoking and will protect their addiction. Sound familiar? Addictions can be deadly. Remember when I talked about the warning signs and how I, or you, as far as that's concerned, may ignore them? You know it might kill you, but you won't stop. She admits it's a problem and how badly he wants to quit. This is when I said to myself, "Now you are beginning to see how the addict feels," and I don't mean that in a bad way.

While she was in the hospital for those couple of days, I felt I was put through the toughest ordeal of my recovery. The ordeal was being home alone and dealing with the thought of using. In the past, this would have been an ideal moment. These are the times the addiction raises its ugly head, it calls me by name... "Jimmy, how are you doing?... I see you're home alone... just you and me, Jimmy... your wife's in the hospital, and you've got a little money in your pocket... how long has it been since you used? What? Nearly a year!! You deserve a little pat on the back, and besides, you're only going to spend 20 dollars... You don't need to worry about taking the piss test. You're off from work... I admit I admire you, Jimmy, for the fact that you've been going to meetings, attending church, and staying clean... You need a little break... what do you think, Jimmy?" I, Jimmy, think no!!!

This is when you are at your weakest, but keep in mind the addiction will get you on your strongest day if you let your guard down. Think it through all the way to the other side. What do I gain that I have not gained before by using it? Nothing, nothing but misery.

Nearly 12 months have passed since I started this journey to recovery. I tried my best to keep a journal by writing down some of the back stories and some of my testimonies that affected me, whether they were positive or negative. Writing down some of the back stories and some of the day-to-day circumstances would give me an opportunity to see my progress as I live it. Also, it awakened my thoughts on past events in my life. Some are bittersweet, some are just downright shameful, but they are all the truth. There are things I wish had never happened, but the reality is that they did. Keeping a journal helps you follow the steps in the program. It also assists me with steps four and five of the program. I do have some inventory issues to adress. Sometimes, I feel I have completed step five before I get to step four (see AA book on steps). I have done a lot of admitting concerning my wrongs. Most treatment centers finish steps 1, 2, and 3 while you are in the treatment center, but some you have to complete as you go through life in a timely manner.

The NA (Narcotics Anonymous) is a 12-step program just like the AA (Alcoholics Anonymous). The difference is that one deals with stimulants and opioids, the other deals with alcohol. The principles are the same:

1- Admitting to being powerless over the addiction,

2- Making amends whenever possible, and

3- Being part of a support group.

I will not mention the steps in my story due to copyright infringements. However, these steps can be found in any AA or NA book. Some addicts in the program had problems with step 1. Not wanting to admit their life had become unmanageable. That was me. It seems so easy, but I have seen addicts struggle with steps 1, 2, and 3. My biggest struggle was steps 1 and 3. Step 2 was a no-brainer for me. I always believed in God, but somehow over the years, I lost the connection with God. I felt I had hit rock bottom from a spiritual standpoint. Always having a feeling of emptiness and a void. Step 3 to me was my lack of know-how. I would go as far as to say that I did not want to know how. I did not want to give up control of my life, but in the same process, I had given up control of my life to crack cocaine, sick thinking, and logic. I wanted to live my life on my own terms. Now, when I hear that famous song entitled "I Did It My Way", I quickly remind myself, so did I, and every time I did it my way, my life went the other way. My way did not work for me, Frank Sinatra. In this life, you can have a good life or a bad life. It all depends on how you apply yourself.

You have heard the saying, Willpower and free will. My life was controlled by addiction. The only real determination I had at one time was to continue to use, and I would say I am not alone in this thinking behavior. I would imagine thousands of users have that same feeling. I heard addicts who were in recovery talk about having thoughts of wanting to use in their dreams; welcome to the club, so do I. As long as you don't put it into action, you are safe. The program is not put in place to stop you from thinking, but to change your way of thinking. Change your thinking process. You are going to have dreams and thoughts. I have been told to think things through all the way to the other side. If you are really serious about your recovery, you will find a reason not to use. It's a slow process, but it works. Sometimes, only others can see the rewards, and sometimes only you can see them. When you start seeing them, you are healing. My days now are filled with less turmoil. Everything is coming a little easier.

I often ask myself how different my life would have been had I not gotten involved in doing crack cocaine. Would I have been a better person if I hadn't thought I was a bad person now? I just did things that didn't align with a normal lifestyle. Would I have seen things the way I see them now, was this a wake-up call? I feel humbled in my life now. It's not a day that goes by that I don't think about the what-ifs and the why-nots. But I don't dwell on it. I push forward, knowing every day is leading me into the known and the unknown. We all know what awaits us at the end of this life, death. Crack cocaine is a form of living death. Why was I rushing it? I don't know. Crack does kill, but it tricks you into believing you are living a good life. I have seen firsthand how this drug has affected people's lives.

How it has destroyed lives, family, relationships, communities, this list goes on and on. I know personally of people who have fallen from grace. I know personally of people who have died from their continued use of crack cocaine.

I only talk about what I know, and I know these facts to be true. There were people in my circle during my days of using who are no longer here; they are in the ground, they are dead. I knew young ladies who were beautiful on the outside, and now some of them are unrecognizable. Most of their teeth and hair are missing, and I am sure there are other health problems. Crack cocaine is a lifestyle changer. My heart goes out to anyone who suffers from any addiction, no matter what it might be. It is not easy to recover unless you want it. You've got to want recovery as bad as you wanted the drug or whatever you are addicted to. Remember all those changes you went through to get your drugs; you've got to go through some changes to recover. There are two types of changes. The good changes and the bad changes. If you are an addict, you have been through the bad changes, and if you are in recovery, you are going through the good changes, and that's a good thing.

You've got to want it; otherwise, it won't work. The recovery program works if it's a well-run program and you are really serious about getting clean. You have your support groups, you have your meetings, you have a good program. I say to you, allow it to work, get involved, participate; it can't work without you working it.

On January 29[th,] 2004, I received my 1-year pin. 6 months later, I received my 18-month pin. I am very proud of these achievements. It gives me great fulfillment in my life. Having completed something that was very, very important to me. I know this is just the beginning of another journey. I thank God for all the people who were placed in my path, and I mean the good as well as the bad. I feel the bad people were a test, some I failed. My mother, who raised me, said, "Don't go running with bad company, they will get you in trouble, and it's all kinds of trouble out there." I also must acknowledge that no one put a crack pipe in my mouth and lit it; I did that on my own. My bad choices interrupted my so-called normal life. I place my one-year coin and my 18 coin beside the pine cone I received from Highland Ridge; They are constant reminders of where my life is going, not where I have been. If you are in recovery or know of someone who is an addict, or maybe just struggling with life. I certainly hope I have written some things that might help someone. Whether you are an addict or not, we are all in this world together. We are to help one another whenever we see fit. You can't help everybody, but help the ones you can. For the last 18 months, I am living proof, and I thank those who helped me along the way. You can continue to walk in the dark or join me and walk in the light, and the light is the light of my higher power, God.

Where I have been, only darkness triumphs. This final chapter of this story was the hardest for me to write. I would like to end my story the same way I started, and this is with a letter. When I was in Highland Ridge, one of my counselors, Rochelle, had an assignment for my wife and me to do. She wanted us to list our boundaries. She also wanted Brenda to write a letter telling me how she felt about my drugs. While Brenda was in the hospital having surgery, I kept myself busy by doing house chores. While cleaning up the closet, I came across this letter written in her own words. I would like to share this letter with you.

Dear Jimmy,

I hope this letter finds you doing fine, or at least better, and that you are really making an effort to recover this time. Rochelle and I talked today; she wanted me to write down some things about what you had done over the years that had an effect on me, hurt me, and this family during your drug use, so I told her I would. Don't think I am trashing you during family sessions; it's just the way I have felt. I think when we first got married, it was because I was in love with you. I could not handle lying, going to the car wash, and not showing up for days without a phone call or anything. I had children who were at home then, and I saw them hurt, and honestly, I was so hurt I really did not know how to deal with them, and you. But as time went on, I became aware of just how bad things were. I vowed, because you are a good man, to stand beside you and to learn as much about your disease as possible, and help all of us. Let me tell you, I was a lot dumber and new in the marriage, not to believe. But as the years went by, you have made me a smarter person. I am going to now say and write the thing that really hurt me, without going through everything, ok. I guess the first was early in our marriage, the lying and worrying almost killed me. I guess when I had that heart attack, I was afraid I would die any second, and right after that, I got out of the hospital, you went and stayed and spent the insurance money on drugs instead of paying the doctors who saved my life.

Working and not having a ride home or waiting for you to bring your car, which you left down the road, you're calling, and I could not say where you were, or how long you would be gone. That was terrible when your job called. I mean, it was pretty obvious no matter what I say. I know you had friends at the railroad to help you; if not, you probably would have been fired. Then I remembered some one from the railroad calls me and tell me you are in Oklahoma at a state fair having a good ole time and I was here lying my butt off to keep your job. When you finally did call me, you acted like I was the one with the problem. There was the time when I was at work and you took Shane to the Mall. And told him you would be right back. He was thirteen years old, and you left him there. Five hours later, he is upset because he can't believe you just left him there. I had to leave work, carry him home, and talk and explain. How do you explain that? Everybody is home, thinking you are dead or something. Three days later, you show up with an "I'm sorry." That hurt me to see you do my child that way, and really, so many things could have happened to Shane. There was the time you took me to the hospital, and I had to have emergency surgery. As soon as they knocked me out, you were gone; you left me. The next day, the kids came to see me, and as they were coming to the hospital (where they caught a ride), they saw you at a pay phone calling someone (not me). They made Calvin look at something on the other side so that he would not see you. They knew what you were doing and did not want you to know. Of course, they were taking care of themselves. Shane was 13, and Seth was 10. As by then I did not get the message, you did not really care bout us, you left me at the hospital again. During all of this time, you completely quit having anything to do with me. I felt more like a sister than a wife because you always put me down. At first, I thought it was because I had gained weight. I tried different hairstyles and did anything I could, but it just got worse. I got so depressed. You have been like living with a stranger at times. You protect those people, and you've never been there for me. Now, if you cry, you want all the compassion you can get. If I cry over you or anything, you leave me alone, or you would really be mean and tell me to stop crying, and you walk out. You just have a good reason. When I got so depressed, I couldn't do anything but cry, it's mostly about us, and all of this.

The other thing that hurt me is Seth coming home this summer (2002) after being overseas for several months. You built him up so much about going fishing with you, and you didn't even go. You go to Walmart to get fishing gear and don't show up for two days; that hurts Seth. He had gone and bought his stuff to go fishing and waited for you as it got dark; his face dropped. I could hardly stand it. They all love you so much; he could not wait to spend time with you after being overseas for several months. He missed his family, especially you; you hurt him so badly; I will never forgive you.

Again, I deal with it, and you come in and say the same old, same old and expect everybody just to pick up and forget that you ruined Seth's vacation. Now, he is back over there in a much worse situation, and you might just wish you had taken that trip. Jimmy, you have done things to Drake (your grandson). He is just 6 years old, but believe me, he is catching on real quick. I am not a pro at this, and I won't let you do this to him that way. I am stronger now than I was when the kids were small. Let's not forget Christmas, for which I got blamed and was grabbed up and treated so badly. I was wrong; what I did was wrong. I didn't care because you had been gone, and I just could not deal with it anymore. I tried to hurt you; instead, I ended up hurting myself. You kind of did that, too. It had gotten to the point where I did not care. So I did something stupid, but man, did you pitch a fit and make me feel lower than I already did. You put bruises on my arm when you grabbed me. Now, when you screw up, you don't ever want me to raise my voice.

Jimmy, I have enjoyed my weeks since you have been gone, and I feel so much better. I don't mean that in an ugly way; I just understand and know you are okay and don't have to worry all night and day, and I listen to you with stories when you decide to come home. I know it's been the same for you, just peace. I think when you call, you are excited about everything, and you expect me to respond with all the mushy stuff, and I am not excited at all. I hope you can understand. I need the time to get myself together. I need to be alone. I have peace, and it feels so good. I just cannot do it anymore.

If this does help you and you really don't want this, we won't be together. I am really prepared to divorce you if things go back the way they were. I think you are basically a wonderful person with a huge problem, and you have made it worse. If you continue to protect people, places, and things you won't have to, I will give them to you so you can carry on. I like it calm and peaceful; it's great. I won't trash you. We will just come to an agreement. If I start getting depressed because I think I am not a woman or don't feel like one or a "True Wife," I will just go and try to be happy. You being gone is like a concrete block being lifted off me. My thoughts are much clearer.

Don't be afraid to tell me about how you feel. I suspect you feel the same.

Brenda

Fast forward to the year 2024, the present day. A lot of things have happened in the last 22 years. All the kids and grandkids that Brenda and I raised are grown, married, and have families of their own. God has blessed me to see them grow up and start their own families. Drakes, our grandson, did a tour of military duty, served his time, and got out. Now he is married, has a family of three, and is a police officer, and he loves it. Drake's sister, Matt, as I call her, is fulfilling her life dream of becoming an RN or Vet; she loves animals. Matt has the newest member of the family, Little Norah, and Myles, Drake's brother, who just graduated from high school—hugs and kisses to their mom, Sonia, who has done a wonderful job raising her kids.

Seth, the youngest son who was in the Navy, has relocated out of state. He and I spent a lot of time fishing, we talked about the fishing trip that I screwed up years ago. I know Seth, and that didn't sit well with him, but one thing about Seth is that he has a forgiving heart, judges you on your present actions, and will always give you his honest feelings about any matter. Several years ago, he took me to my first Pro Football game and Pro Basketball game, all on the same weekend. Yeah, beat that. I played a lot of softball when his mother and I got married, and he was always with me. I remember playing softball in Oklahoma in 1995, the year of the Oklahoma City bombing; Seth and I went and visited the bombing site. He was always my riding buddy, whether fishing or softball. He bought a place in Virginia that had a pond behind it; I tell you, I have never had so much fun fishing off the bank in my life; I really hate that he moved. He and I talk 2 to 3 times a week, every week. I am so proud of Seth and his lovely family.

Shane, Seth's brother, lives in the city where I live. We talk quite often; he is currently working as a Supervisor at a Millrite plant near me. He is so busy working that he doesn't see his children very much, and Jonathan and Mandi, the other children, live in a town about 2 hours' drive away.

Brenda would have loved this; she really believed in family. Brenda and I had some wonderful years together once I got my act together. This was achieved by changing my negative actions and by Brenda being receptive to the changes I made. Brenda and the children really became my support team. Their main concern about me was that I get better. Picking up the grandkids from school was such a joy. That was my therapy every day. I regained the trust I had lost in myself, and I felt the same way about my coworkers.

Trust and being reliable were important to me. I had lost trust, both at home and at work. By the way, I made amends with one of the church members concerning the money I had taken back when I was using. I paid the church their money back with interest. My final fate on that matter is in God's final judgment.

Brenda and I had our little piece of Paradise. We went on vacation every year and took the kids and grandkids. As long as there was a beach, they were happy. We even spent a week in Vegas. Brenda and I were married for over 25 years. Our marriage had its ups and downs, more ups than downs.

On October 5, 2017, Brenda passed away somewhat unexpectedly. She had been having a few health issues, but no one expected this; she was 62 years old. Every year from 2017 til now, we gather at her grave site on her birthday, July 5th, to do a balloon release and to honor her life. In the first year, only 5 or 6 of us showed up. But, this last year, 2024, we had 24 people attend; it gives us as a family a chance to get together and enjoy one another and introduce her great-grandkids to their great-grandmother so she won't be forgotten. We all love her... I especially love her because she believed in me... She would not let me give up on myself. She had my back.

I am 72 years old, retired, and still widowed. I have not smoked a cigarette in 23 years, and I have not done crack cocaine in 22 years and counting. I stayed clean and sober for a total of 18 months. I consider myself sober today because I am staying away from addictive substances. I do not consider myself clean, but I do have a sober thinking process. You may not agree, and you are entitled to your opinion. Yes, I have my occasional beer and wine during certain celebrations, depending on my mood. I don't drink hard liquor, but I will make an occasional toast with the fellows I shoot pool with. I don't keep beer around. A six-pack of my favorite beer may last all week, and I keep wine in my wine racks for guests... I have accepted these things, as they all required TIME...

Thanks for reading my story.